The Chef's Répertoire

AMERICAN TECHNICAL PUBLISHERS
ORLAND PARK, ILLINOIS 60467-5756

Chef Gui Alinat

1 2 3 4 5 6 7 8 9 – 10 – 9 8 7 6 5 4 3 2 1

Printed in the United States of America

ISBN 978-0-8269-4235-7

 This book is printed on recycled paper.

To my beautiful, talented children,
Julian and Brune,
without whom nothing is possible.

This book is also dedicated to
Fall lunches at Le Mas du Langoustier
on the island of Porquerolles, France.

Contents

The author and publisher appreciate the technical reviews provided by these prestigious culinary artists:

Chef Marie-Annick Courtier (www.chefmarie.com)

Chef Ariane Daguin (www.dartagnan.com)

Chef Jaden Hair (www.SteamyKitchen.com)

Pastry Chef Beth Karam-Putt (www.sweetsisterscakes.com)

Chef Ray "Dr. BBQ" Lampe (www.drbbq.com)

Chef J. Hugh McEvoy (President, Chicago Research Chefs)

The author and publisher are grateful for the images provided by the following:

Daniel NYC (pages 109, 113, and 135)

Florida Department of Agriculture and Consumer Services, Bureau of Seafood and Aquaculture Marketing (page 63)

Idaho Potato Commission (pages 57 and 117)

The Beef Checkoff (pages 25 and 71)

Perdue Foodservice, Perdue Farms Incorporated (page 71)

Wisconsin Milk Marketing Board (page 37)

It is exciting to have young Chef Gui Alinat choose to pen a new répertoire of the foods prepared and served in a range of American restaurants, from casual to fine dining. I readily agreed to write the foreword for a new book inspired by *Le Répertoire de La Cuisine*, as my copy of the professional chefs' bible has served me so well. That old inventory of "chef's reminders" was invaluable as I worked in world-renown kitchens in England, France, and Spain with legendary Chefs Gagnaire, Mosimann, Guerard, and Blanc before becoming a successful chef/restaurateur back here in America.

Given that I started my humble culinary career cooking hamburgers and now, 32 years later, have the privilege and honor of operating four upscale restaurants in the greater Chicago area, I was eager to introduce the written work of a chef who is making waves both online and in the professional kitchen. I sincerely applaud Chef Gui's research into the vast array of dishes that America consumes in order to select the entries found in *The Chef's Répertoire*.

While all culinary professionals enjoy creating unexpected flavor combinations to place on the table, we are not masters at naming dishes. Gui's decision to exclude self-describing dishes that literally tell you what is being served is so welcome. Instead, Gui lists dishes with names that do not necessarily describe their ingredients and hence are harder for chefs and professional cooks to memorize.

As an accomplished cookbook author of seven books, I know how much personal time, dedication, and sacrifice it takes to create a useful and meaningful book that you are proud to see promoted online and in bookstores. Chef Gui's first book is definitely one he can be proud of, and I believe that it will be well-received by professional chefs and culinary enthusiasts alike. Gui has created a quick-reference inventory that every American working in the hospitality industry should own.

By maintaining the small trim size, *The Chef's Répertoire* conveniently fits in your chef's apron pocket, just like the original répertoire. With Gui's book however, several user-friendly improvements have been made. For example, thumb tabs appear on every page to make it easy to find the sections: Stocks & Base Sauces, Sauces, Soups, Appetizers, Eggs, Fish & Seafood, Meats & Poultry, Pasta, Salads, Sandwiches, Sides, and Desserts. The entries within each category are listed alphabetically and most entries provide a pronunciation guide and country of origin in addition to the recipe description. On rare occasions, some ingredient amounts are given. As necessary, a few entries are listed in more than one category.

The Chef's Répertoire is the new, modern chef's bible and every practicing chef, culinary student, chef educator, and cooking enthusiast should own a copy of this remarkable and user-friendly book of recipe reminders.

Bon appétit,

Rick Tramonto

Executive Chef/Partner TRU
Culinary Director, Tramonto Cuisine & Tramonto Steakhouse

I could probably write a whole book acknowledging all the people who made *The Chef's Répertoire* possible. First and foremost, I am forever indebted to Chef Rick Tramonto for his remarkable generosity in writing the foreword. His compassion and professionalism are beyond words. Seeing my name next to his on the book jacket is an honor, and humbling. I hope to one day "pay it forward" by extending the same kindness to another young chef's first book.

I am also proud to acknowledge the contributions of the talented and internationally known group of chefs who were gracious enough to review my book prior to publication: Chefs Ariane Daguin, Marie-Annick Courtier, Ray "Dr. BBQ" Lampe, Jaden Hair, J. Hugh McEvoy, and Pastry Chef Beth Karam-Putt. Their suggestions and comments greatly contributed to the quality of this book.

There is also a special group of Tampa Bay individuals who were my clients before becoming my friends. Thanks to their constant business and enlightened advice, my catering team was able to become a culinary landmark in the Tampa Bay area. I am especially grateful to Marc Jacobson, Greg Gregory, Harry Teasley, Lorna Taylor, Pamela and Michael Adams, Tamara and Ron Broadrick, Dimity and Mark Carlson, Jere Tolton and Jory Williams, Christine Laramée and John Kilgore, Loyd Pettigrew and Carol Vance, Beth and Birge Sigety, Jim Sirna, the eight boys from the dinner club, and many others who have made my path easier.

Most importantly, I could not have written this book without the extraordinary network of family and friends who always believed in me and who supported my work with continuous encouragement. A special thank you to my parents Michel and Chantal, my talented brother Chef Romain Alinat, Janis and Bob Gallo, Willy and Rosangela Brevet, Laura Boyd, Esther Romeyn, Marcel Aumann, and Laterika Jelks.

Finally, I would like to express my appreciation to my publisher, whose expectations and methods are impressive. This may be the most professional team I have ever met, in or outside the kitchen.

While I thank all members of the American Technical Publishers staff who assisted with the production and publication of *The Chef's Répertoire*, I am especially grateful to my editor, Cathy Scruggs, who recognized this book's value to the field of culinary arts and helped to give my work a voice. Her encouragement, intuition, and compassion kept me focused when writing was most challenging. Special thanks go to Catherine Mini, who copyedited all of the pronunciations and origins as well as the descriptions. I also would like to recognize Jim Clarke's artful execution of the book jacket and interior design, which make this book so pleasing to the eye.

It is my sincerest hope that this book will offer direction to those new to the culinary profession and serve as a familiar friend for seasoned professionals who share a passion for cooking and serving culinary delights.

—Gui Alinat, CEC

Introduction

In 1986, I started chef school in France during the Nouvelle cuisine frenzy. Escoffier's classic French cuisine was still the standard. At the time, the 1914 edition of *Le Répertoire de La Cuisine* was quite literally our pocket reference. In spite of its small size, the répertoire, or "Le Gringoire et Saulnier" as it was often called, condensed the quasi-entirety of Auguste Escoffier's *Le Guide Culinaire*. We apprentice chefs would take the répertoire into the kitchen so we could refresh our memories if we were challenged on the spot. What is a potage Saint-Germain? What makes a Mornay? And what goes into Dubarry?

Twenty-five years after making my first mirepoix, classical French cuisine is still with us, but these dishes are much less prominent on menus today. Nouvelle cuisine, after a turbulent beginning, has provided an extraordinary basis for the creativity craved by professional chefs. Thanks to Nouvelle, chefs are no longer tied to ancient recipes and are now empowered to create dishes according to their own artistic inclinations.

Recently, the culinary landscape has been undergoing another revolution. Following the Spanish masters, cuisine is being transformed globally by the avant-garde vision of talented European and American chefs, with an emphasis on technology and molecular gastronomy. What remains unchanged is the challenge of naming a dish.

Many concepts go into the naming of a dish, but we distinguish between only two types of names. There are descriptive names, like seared scallops with ginger-sake reduction, and there are nondescriptive names, such as beef Wellington with béarnaise sauce and pommes cocotte. It is fair to say that to the novice, the former dish provides better information in regard to ingredients and techniques than the latter.

Naming dishes has a long history. Who gave the first dish a nondescriptive name is not known. But the grande cuisine of Antonin Carême (1784-1833), and later the classical cuisine of Auguste Escoffier (1846-1935), tremendously increased the number of named dishes, and *Le Répertoire de la Cuisine* listed almost all of them.

Regionalization, local classics, and celebrity chefs further developed nondescriptive names for dishes. And global cuisine includes dishes with names from many languages that we often do not speak, yet professional chefs are expected to know how to prepare thousands of these dishes.

The Chef's Répertoire addresses this challenge. With it, professional and home chefs alike have a practical reference that serves as a reminder of classic nondescriptive dishes, whether regional or international, casual or fine dining, classical or modern. I tried to describe what makes a dish authentic through careful research. However, there are often regional or cultural variations. For instance, there are as many types of vinaigrette as there are chefs. Similarly, some esoteric dishes such as red-eye gravy and bibimbap are included because they do appear on some American restaurant menus and as online recipes. I did not include self-describing dishes because professional chefs know what goes into a cream of mushroom soup or a seared filet mignon with a Port and shallot reduction.

As food and technology constantly evolve and the vast common knowledge of the profession continues to expand, chefs need a place to look up classic dishes on the fly, refresh their memories, and quickly respond to the challenges of the professional kitchen.

The Chef's Répertoire identifies, classifies, clarifies, and synthesizes the bulk of the classic dishes that compose modern cuisine in America.

Enjoy!

—Gui Alinat, CEC

Using the Répertoire

The Chef's Répertoire is not a dictionary or a cookbook. It is more than definitions or a compilation of recipes. It is an inventory of classic dishes that compose modern cuisine in America arranged in such a way that it makes them easy to find. Each entry, written in a chef's vocabulary, describes the natural sequence of a dish in a few concise phrases. Thus, readers are expected to have some culinary knowledge. While the novice may be challenged when following the progression of each classic dish as listed, the professional or serious home chef will navigate easily.

The book contains over 1100 entries divided into 12 sections and listed alphabetically. Key culinary terms are listed at the beginning of the book, and thumb tabs clearly identify each section. A complete list of all the dishes is located at the back of the book, with page numbers for each entry.

Origin   Pronunciation

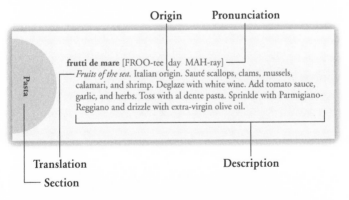

frutti de mare [FROO-tee day MAH-ray]
— *Fruits of the sea.* Italian origin. Sauté scallops, clams, mussels, calamari, and shrimp. Deglaze with white wine. Add tomato sauce, garlic, and herbs. Toss with al dente pasta. Sprinkle with Parmigiano-Reggiano and drizzle with extra-virgin olive oil.

Pasta

Translation   Description

Section

Some dishes are listed in more than one section. For instance, bouillabaisse is a fish entrée but could also be served as a soup, so it is listed in both "Fish & Seafood" and in "Soups." Breads are not included, as baking is a separate topic best reserved for bakers.

The Chef's Répertoire

Key Culinary Terms

à blanc [ah BLAHNK]
French. *Until white.*

à brun [ah BROO]
French. *Until brown.*

à la [ah lah]
French. *In the style of.*

à la minute [ah lah mee-NOOT]
French. *At the last minute.*

a la plancha [ah lah PLAN-chuh]
Spanish. *On a griddle.*

al dente [al DEN-tay]
Italian. *To the teeth.* Cooked until tender but still firm.

alla [a-lah]
Italian. *In the style of.*

au beurre
French. *With butter.*

aspic
A clear jelly made from stock or fruit juices and thickened with gelatin.

beurre manié [burr mahn-YAY]
French. *Kneaded butter.* A mixture of equal parts of butter and flour that is used to thicken sauces. Similar to a roux.

bouquet garni [BOO-kay gahr-NEE]
French. Small bundle of herbs tied with a string, such as bay leaf, parsley, thyme, or a combination of these and others.

emulsify
To mix an oil-based liquid and a water-based liquid until homogeneous. Emulsions can be stable or unstable.

essence
A concentrated flavor that is extracted, usually by infusion.

filé powder
A thickener made from ground dried sassafras leaves.

fines herbes [feen AIRB]
French. A mixture of fresh herbs, usually parsley, chervil, tarragon and chives.

garam masala
Hindi. *Hot mixture.* A mixture of powdered peppercorns, cloves, cinnamon, green and black cardamom, and cumin.

jus lié [ZHOO lee-ay]
French. Slightly thickened cooking juices.

monter [MOHN-tay]
French. To whisk or build up in order to thicken.

nappé [NA-pay]
French. To coat the back of a spoon.

paellera [pigh-AIR-uh]
Spanish. *Paella pan.*

pastis [PAHS-tees]
French. Anise-flavored French liqueur.

Stocks & Base Sauces

béchamel [bay-shah-MEL]

French origin. Start with a warm flour-butter roux. Add cold milk. Bring to a boil while stirring to control consistency. Simmer 25 minutes. (If desired, add chopped onions, bacon, or mushrooms.)

beef stock

Roast beef bones until dark brown. Sauté mirepoix and brown. (If desired, add parsley and mushrooms.) Add tomato concentrate. Cover with cold water and deglaze. Add thyme, bay leaf, and garlic. Simmer 6 to 8 hours. Strain through sieve. Defat when cold.

blonde roux [roo]

Melt 1 volume of butter. Add 1 volume of flour and mix until homogeneous. Cook until roux changes consistency and becomes beige in color. Avoid scorching. Use to thicken white sauce and soup.

brown roux [roo]

Melt 1 volume of butter. Add 1 volume of flour and mix until homogeneous. Cook until roux changes consistency and is caramel in color. Avoid scorching. Use to thicken brown sauce or gumbo.

brown sauce (see espagnole)

chicken stock

Roast chicken bones. Sauté mirepoix but do not brown. (If desired, add parsley and mushrooms.) Cover with cold water. Add thyme, bay leaf, and garlic. Simmer 1 hour. Strain through sieve. Defat when cold.

court bouillon [kort BOOL-yahn]

French origin. Combine equal parts of white wine and fish stock or shellfish stock. Add mirepoix. Add spices such as cloves, coriander, fennel seeds, and bay leaves. Salt and pepper to taste. (If desired, add milk and lemon juice or vinegar.) Bring to a boil and use to poach fish.

demi-glace [DUH-mee-glahs]

French origin. Make veal stock. Add brown roux. Reduce by half to achieve desired consistency.

duxelles [dook-sel]

French origin. Sauté chopped shallots and chopped mushrooms. (If desired, flambé with cognac.) Deglaze with white wine. Reduce until dry. Salt and pepper to taste.

espagnole [es-pah-NYOHL]
 French origin. Start with brown roux. Add veal stock or water.
 Reinforce with veal or beef bones and meat, mirepoix, and seasonings.
 Simmer. Add tomato paste or puréed tomatoes. Reduce to sauce
 consistency.

fish stock (see fumet)

fumet [fyoo-MAY]
 French origin. Sweat mirepoix with diced leeks. Sauté fish bones until
 colorless. Cover with half cold water and half white wine. (If desired,
 add parsley and mushrooms.) Add peppercorns. Simmer 30 minutes.
 Infuse 30 minutes. Strain through thin sieve.

hollandaise [HOL-un-dayz]
 Dutch origin. Start with cracked pepper and vinegar. Reduce until
 almost dry. Add egg yolks. Slowly incorporate fresh butter, alternating
 with small quantities of cold water. Whisk until homogeneous. Finish
 with lemon juice. Salt and pepper to taste. (If desired, add cayenne
 pepper.) Serve warm.

lobster stock
 Roast lobster shells. Sauté shells with mirepoix and diced leeks until
 colorless. Cover with half cold water and half white wine. (If desired,
 add parsley and mushrooms.) Add peppercorns. Simmer 30 minutes.
 Infuse 30 minutes. Strain through thin sieve.

mayonnaise
 French origin. Start with 1 egg yolk. Mix in salt and pepper to taste.
 Add Dijon mustard, vinegar, or lemon juice. Whisk in vegetable oil
 slowly (1 cup per egg yolk) until homogeneous and thick. (If desired,
 add cayenne pepper.)

mirepoix [meer-PWAH]
 French origin. Diced onions, carrots, and celery in a ratio of 2:1:1. (If
 desired, add bay leaf or diced bacon.) May or may not be sautéed.

red sauce (see tomato sauce)

tomato concassée [kon-kah-SAY]
 French origin. Sauté diced onions. Add skinless, seedless, diced
 tomatoes. Add garlic, bay leaf, and sugar for acidity correction. Salt
 and pepper to taste. Reduce until slightly dry.

tomato sauce

Sauté mirepoix and garlic. (If desired, add bacon or pancetta until slightly brown.) Add tomato concentrate. (If desired, add roux.) Deglaze with white or red wine. Add peeled and seeded ripe tomatoes. Reduce. Add sugar for acidity correction. Add herbs such as bay leaf, thyme, rosemary, oregano, and basil. Salt and pepper to taste. Simmer for hours. (If desired, process until smooth.)

veal stock

Roast veal bones. Sauté mirepoix and brown. (If desired, add parsley and mushrooms.) Add tomato concentrate. Cover with cold water. Add thyme, bay leaf, and garlic. Simmer 6 to 8 hours. Strain through fine sieve. Defat when cold.

velouté [vuh-loo-TAY]

French origin. Start with clear chicken stock. (If desired, use fish or veal stock.) Thicken with blonde roux.

vinaigrette [vee-nuh-GRET]

French origin. Mix 3 parts oil and 1 part vinegar. Add salt and pepper. (If desired, add herbs, spices, shallots, onions, Dijon mustard, raspberries, or Champagne.)

white roux [roo]

Melt 1 volume of butter. Add 1 volume of flour until homogeneous. Cook until roux changes consistency and is cream in color. Avoid scorching. Use to thicken white sauce and soup.

white sauce (see béchamel)

The Chef's Répertoire Sauces

achiote [ah-chee-OH-tay] (see recado)

africaine [a-free-KEN]
Start with espagnole. Add African spices such as melegueta peppers, cloves, cardamom, nutmeg, and turmeric.

agrodolce [a-groh-DOHL-chay]
Italian origin. Caramelize sugar. Add vinegar. (If desired, add fruit juice.) Finish with stock. Reduce to sauce consistency. Salt and pepper to taste.

aigre-douce [ay-gruh DOOS] (see gastrique)

aïoli [ay-OH-lee]
French origin (Southern). Crush garlic in mortar or food processor. Add mustard. (If desired, add cooked potato.) Salt and pepper to taste. Add 1 egg yolk and slowly add 1 cup of olive oil. Emulsify. Finish with lemon juice and cayenne pepper.

à la king
American origin. Sear chicken. Reserve. Sauté mushrooms, green peppers, and pimientos. Deglaze with white wine. Reduce. Add chicken stock. Reduce. Finish with cream and reduce. Add salt and pepper. (If desired, flambé with sherry and monter au beurre.)

Albert [al-BAIR]
British origin. Start with clear beef broth. Grate horseradish root. Thicken with cream and egg yolks. Served with braised or poached beef.

allemande [a-luh-MAHND]
French origin. Thicken a classic velouté with egg yolks.

allïoli [ay-lee-YOHL-ee]
Spanish origin (Catalonia). Crush garlic in mortar or food processor. Add mustard. (If desired, add cooked potato.) Salt and pepper to taste. Slowly add 1 cup of olive oil. Emulsify. Finish with lemon juice and cayenne pepper.

américaine [a-may-ree-KEN]
French origin. Sauté lobster, crab, or shrimp shells with mirepoix and tomato concentrate. (If desired, flambé with cognac or sherry.) Deglaze with white wine. Add fish stock. Reduce. Thicken with roux or egg yolks. (If desired, add cream to soften.)

andalouse [ahn-dah-LOOZ]
French origin. Rouille plus tomato paste or reduced tomato concassée.

applesauce
British origin. Cook peeled apples with a little sugar and cinnamon. Process until smooth.

arrabiata [A-ruh-BYAHT-ah]
Italian origin. Traditionally served with penne pasta. Start with red wine tomato sauce. Reinforce with fresh basil, chili peppers, and fresh chopped parsley for presentation.

asian barbecue sauce
Start a caramel with sugar. Add hoisin sauce, rice vinegar, Asian fish sauce, soy sauce, honey, minced shallots, grated ginger, and Chinese five-spice. Simmer. Chill.

au jus [oh ZHOO]
French origin. Roast a piece of meat (beef, veal, or chicken). Reserve the meat. Caramelize the cooking juices. Deglaze with water or wine. Salt and pepper to taste.

au poivre [oh PWAHV-ruh]
Crust beef with cracked peppercorns. Sear meat. Reserve. Sauté chopped shallots and flambé with cognac. Add white wine. Reduce. Add demi-glace. Add cream. Reduce to sauce consistency. (If desired, monter au beurre.)

aurore [oh ROR]
French origin. Start with a supreme sauce. Add tomato concasseé. Process if needed.

bacon mayonnaise
Make mayonnaise but replace oil with rendered bacon fat.

balchao [bal-show]
Portuguese-Indian origin. Process malt vinegar, tamarind paste, dried chilies, cumin seeds, black peppercorns, cloves, turmeric, garlic, fresh ginger, and cinnamon. Chill. Pickle for a few days.

balsamic reduction
Reduce chopped shallots, cracked pepper, stock or pan-drippings, and balsamic vinegar to sauce consistency. Strain if desired.

barbecue sauce; barbeque sauce
American origin. Regional variations. Sauté garlic, onions, and bell peppers. Add ketchup, tomato sauce, cider vinegar, Worcestershire, hot sauce, liquid smoke, molasses, brown sugar, mustard, and black pepper. Add water, beer, or wine for desired consistency. Simmer. Process.

Béarnaise [bair-NEZ]
French origin. Reduce white wine vinegar, tarragon, chopped shallots, coarse peppercorns, and salt. When dry, add egg yolks. Whisk in warm or clarified butter. Finish with lemon juice and chopped tarragon.

béchamel [bay-shah-MEL]
French origin. Start with a warm flour-butter roux. Add cold milk. Bring to a boil while stirring to control consistency. Simmer 25 minutes. (If desired, add chopped onions, bacon, or mushrooms.)

Bercy [BAIR-see]
French origin. Sauté chopped shallots. Add white wine and fish stock. Reduce. Add velouté or demi-glace. Monter au beurre. Finish with chopped parsley.

beurre blanc [burr BLAHNK]
French origin. Reduce shallots, cracked white pepper, and white wine. (If desired, add white vinegar.) Monter au beurre. Salt and pepper to taste. Finish with lemon juice.

beurre noir [burr NWAR]
French origin. Heat butter on low heat until solids turn dark brown. Add lemon juice or vinegar. (If desired, add chopped parsley.)

beurre noisette [burr nwah-ZET]
French origin. Heat butter on low heat until solids turn light brown. Pass through chinois.

bigarade [bee-gah-RAHD]
French origin. Similar to orange sauce. Start with au jus of duck, veal, lamb, or beef. Add orange or lemon juice. Add orange or lemon peel julienne. Monter au beurre. (If desired, add roux for consistency.) Salt and pepper to taste.

bird-eye gravy (see red-eye gravy)

blue cheese dressing
American origin. Mix mayonnaise, sour cream, and blue cheese. Add onion powder, dry mustard, and garlic powder. Salt and pepper to taste. Emulsify.

Bolognese [boh-luh-NYAY-zay]
Italian origin. Sauté onions, garlic, and bacon. Add ground beef and tomato paste. Deglaze with red wine. (If desired, add tomato sauce.) Salt and pepper to taste. Simmer 2 hours.

Bordelaise [bor-duh-LEZ]
French origin. Reduce chopped shallots, coarse peppercorns, thyme, bay leaf, and red Bordeaux wine. Add demi-glace. (If desired, pass through chinois.) Salt and pepper to taste.

bourbon barbecue sauce
Bring ketchup, molasses, bourbon, mustard, hot sauce, Worcestershire, paprika, chopped garlic, and onions to a boil. Process. Chill.

Bourguignonne [boor-gee-NYUN]
French origin. Cover thinly chopped shallots, parsley, thyme, and bay leaves with red wine. (If desired, add mushrooms.) Reduce. Add roux for consistency. (If desired, add cayenne pepper.) Salt and pepper to taste.

bread sauce
Simmer milk with onion and clove. Add fresh white bread. Process. Add cream. Salt and pepper to taste.

brown sauce (see espagnole)

Caesar dressing
Mix Dijon mustard, egg yolk, Worcestershire, lemon juice, extra-virgin olive oil, garlic, and Parmesan. (If desired, add anchovies.) Salt and pepper to taste. Emulsify.

Cajun gravy
Start with dark, thick, spicy brown roux. Add chicken broth or water, paprika, and cayenne pepper. Salt and pepper to taste. Simmer. Correct consistency.

Cajun-style gravy
Sauté chicken gizzards and then chop finely. Return to pan with ground beef, ground pork, green peppers, onions, garlic, and cayenne pepper. Add flour to make a roux. Add beef broth or water. Add cayenne pepper. Salt and pepper to taste. Simmer.

Cambridge
British origin. Process hard-boiled egg yolks, anchovies, capers, and fine herbs such as chives, tarragon, and parsley. Add mustard and vinegar. Whisk in olive oil. Add cayenne pepper. Salt and pepper to taste. Serve chilled.

charcutière [shahr-koo-TYAIR]
French origin. Start with Robert sauce. Add chopped gherkins.

charmoula [CHAHR-moo-lah]
North African origin (Mahgreb). Regional variations. Process toasted cumin, garlic, cilantro, Italian parsley, lemon juice, paprika, and cayenne pepper into a paste. Monter with olive oil. Salt and pepper to taste. Chill. Use as sauce, marinade, or dip.

chasseur [shah-SUR]
French origin. Sauté sliced mushrooms. Add chopped shallots. Deglaze with white wine. Reduce. Add demi-glace. Monter au beurre. (If desired, add chopped parsley.) Salt and pepper to taste.

chaud-froid [shoh-FWAH]
French origin. Add gelatin to velouté. Variation: Add demi-glace, truffles, or Madeira wine.

chevreuil [shev-ROY]
French origin. Variation of roebuck sauce. Sauté mirepoix and venison bits. Add red wine. Reduce. Add demi-glace. (If desired, add cayenne pepper.) Salt and pepper to taste. Serve with venison or other game meat.

chimichurri [chee-mee-CHOO-ree]
Argentine origin. Process garlic, parsley, cilantro, olive oil, sherry vinegar, onions, and capers. Salt and pepper to taste.

chimichurri rojo [chee-mee-CHOO-ree ROH-hoh]
Argentine origin. Mix Jerez vinegar, olive oil, paprika, cayenne pepper, chopped garlic, and ground cumin. Salt and pepper to taste. Serve at room temperature as a sauce, marinade, or dip.

choron [show-RAHN]
French origin. Start with béarnaise. Add tomato concassée or reduced tomato sauce.

chow-chow; chowchow relish
Dry-brine sliced cucumbers or shredded cabbage and reserve. Bring sugar, vinegar, and dry mustard to a boil. Thicken sauce and reserve. Steam diced green tomatoes, green bell peppers, peas, cauliflower, and onions. Add rinsed cucumbers or cabbage. Add sauce. (If desired, preserve relish for later use.)

chutney, cooked
Indian origin. Combine diced fruit (such as mango, apple, pear, or tomato) with sugar, vinegar, Indian spices (such as cinnamon, cloves, curry, cumin, mustrad, or coriander), and an aromatic (such as ginger, garlic, chilies, or raisins). Simmer until mixture is brown and similar to jam. Chill and reserve.

chutney, raw
Indian origin. Combine diced fruit (such as mango, pineapple, or tamarind) with sugar, Indian spices (such as cinnamon, cloves, curry, cumin, or chilies), and fresh herbs (such as mint, cilantro, or tarragon).

cocktail sauce
American origin. Mix ketchup, horseradish, lemon juice, celery salt, and tabasco.

composed butter; compound butter
Many variations. Soften butter at room temperature or in food processor. Add any combination of aromatic elements such as fine herbs, lemon juice, crushed garlic, or anchovy paste. Salt and pepper to taste.

country gravy
Sauté or roast sausage, steak, or chicken. Make a roux with the pan drippings. Add milk like a béchamel. (If desired, add bits of sausage or chicken liver.) Simmer. Salt and pepper to taste.

cranberry sauce
Boil cranberries with water and sugar until berries pop. Add orange zest. Process. Chill.

cream gravy (see country gravy)

Cumberland
Blanch orange and lemon zest. Simmer with red currant jelly, raisins, Port, ginger, cayenne pepper, and water. Thicken with cornstarch. Serve hot or cold with venison or duck.

deviled sauce
English origin. Variation of diable sauce. Start with chopped shallots and vinegar. Reduce until dry. Add demi-glace and tomato concasseé. Process if desired. Add cayenne pepper. Salt and pepper to taste.

diable [dee-AH-bluh]
French origin. Mix chopped shallots and cracked peppercorns with ½ white wine and ½ vinegar. Reduce until dry. Add demi-glace.

Dieppoise [dee-uh-PWAHZ]
Start with normande sauce. Add shrimp. Finish with chopped parsley.

egg gravy
Proceed as with gravy and add a beaten egg at the end. Let the egg coagulate. Serve warm.

espagnole [es-pah-NYOHL]
French origin. Start with brown roux. Add veal stock or water. Reinforce with veal or beef bones and meat, mirepoix, and seasonings. Simmer. Add tomato paste or puréed tomatoes. Reduce to sauce consistency.

financière [feen-ahn-SYAIR]
French origin. Madeira sauce with truffle juice.

French dressing
American origin. Mix 1 cup vegetable oil, 1 cup ketchup, ½ cup vinegar, 1 teaspoon lemon juice, paprika, sugar, salt, and pepper. Emulsify.

gastrique [gah-STREEK]
French origin. Carmelize sugar. Add vinegar. (If desired, add fruit juice.) Finish with stock. Reduce to sauce consistency.

ghee
Indian origin. Heat butter on low heat until solids turn light brown. Pass through chinois.

giblet gravy
Proceed as with gravy. Add cooked chicken or turkey giblets.

Gloucester
British origin. Mix sour cream with mayonnaise, chopped fennel, chives, Worcestershire, lemon juice, and cayenne pepper. Serve chilled.

grand veneur [GRAHN vuh-nur]
French origin. Add venison juices to poivrade sauce. Add gooseberry jelly and cream. Salt and pepper to taste.

gravy
Many variations. Sauté onions. Add flour to make a white or blond roux. Add chicken or beef broth, Worcestershire, and roast turkey or chicken neck and bones. Simmer. Salt and pepper to taste.

green goddess dressing
American origin (California). Mix 1 cup mayonnaise and ½ cup sour cream. Add chopped chives, tarragon, parsley, lemon juice, and anchovies. Salt and pepper to taste. Emulsify.

green tomato salsa
Mexican origin. Mix together diced tomatillos, chopped onions, cilantro, lime juice, and jalapeño peppers. Salt to taste. (If desired, add sugar for acidity correction.)

gribiche [gree-BEESH]
French origin. Start with mayonnaise. Add cooked egg yolks and extra mustard. Add chopped capers, gherkins, and fines herbes. Serve cold.

harissa [HAH-ree-sah]
Tunisian origin. Process chili peppers, garlic, cumin, skinless and seedless tomatoes, caraway and coriander seeds, salt, and olive oil into a paste. (If desired, add roasted, skinless bell peppers.)

hollandaise [HOL-un-dayz]
Dutch origin. Start with cracked pepper and vinegar. Reduce until almost dry. Add egg yolks. Slowly incorporate fresh butter, alternating with small quantities of warm water. Whisk until homogeneous. Finish with lemon juice. Salt and pepper to taste. (If desired, add cayenne pepper.) Serve warm.

horseradish sauce
1. British origin. Grate horseradish and blanch in chicken stock. Make a béchamel sauce. Add horseradish and process with hand blender. Finish with lemon juice. Salt and pepper to taste. Serve hot.
2. American origin. Grate horseradish root. Mix with a little water, white vinegar, and salt. Add sour cream and mayonnaise. (If desired, add chopped chives.) Serve cold.

hunter's sauce (see chasseur)

Italian dressing
American origin. Add equal parts white wine vinegar, water, vegetable oil, and light corn syrup. Add dried parsley, crushed red peppers, and oregano. Salt and pepper to taste. Emulsify.

jitomate [hit-toh-MAH-tay] (see tomato salsa)

ketchup
North American origin. Pureé peeled, seeded tomatoes. Sauté onions. Add puréed tomatoes, tomato paste, brown sugar, vinegar, and salt. Simmer until thick. Process until smooth. Chill.

Louis [LOO-ee] **dressing**
American origin (California). Mix mayonnaise, chili sauce, diced green peppers, scallions, and lemon juice. Salt and pepper to taste.

Lyonnaise [lee-uh-NEZ]
Sauté sliced onions. Deglaze with wine. Reduce. Add demi-glace. Simmer.

Madeira [muh-DEER-uh] **sauce**
Reduce Madeira wine. Add demi-glace. Salt and pepper to taste.

manchamantel [man-CHA-man-tel]
Mexican origin. Process rehydrated ancho chiles, tomatoes, garlic, pineapple, bananas, apples, cinnamon, vinegar, cloves, allspice, and peanut oil. Add water to achieve sauce consistency. Simmer. Serve hot.

marchand de vin [mar-SHAHN duh vehn]
French origin. Sauté onions or shallots. Deglaze with red wine. Reduce to syrup. Add stock. (If desired, add roux.) Reduce. Monter au beurre. Salt and pepper to taste.

marinara
1. Italian origin. Quick-sauté garlic, Mediterranean herbs, and ripe tomatoes in olive oil. Add shellfish, salt, and pepper. (If desired, add sugar for acidity correction.)
2. American origin. Start with tomato sauce. Add chopped garlic, fresh basil, and parsley. Salt and pepper to taste. (If desired, add cayenne pepper and chilies.)

marinière [mah-reen-YAIR]
French origin. Cook mussels with shallots, white wine, butter, and cracked peppercorns. (If desired, add chopped parsley.) Reduce. Monter au beurre.

marsala
Italian origin (Sicily). Regional variations. Sear meat. Reserve. Sauté chopped shallots and mushrooms. Deglaze with Marsala wine. Reduce. Add broth or stock. Reduce. (If desired, add capers and cream. Then reduce again.) Salt and pepper to taste. (If desired, finish with lemon juice and chopped parsley.)

Mayfair dressing
American origin (St. Louis). Process blanched celery and onions. Add garlic and anchovies. Process with 3 whole eggs, Dijon mustard, lemon juice, and 1 cup corn oil. Salt and pepper to taste. Emulsify.

mayonnaise
French origin. Start with 1 egg yolk. Mix in salt and pepper to taste. Add Dijon mustard, vinegar, or lemon juice. Whisk in vegetable oil slowly (1 cup per egg yolk) until homogeneous and thick. (If desired, add cayenne pepper.)

mignonette [min-yuh-NET]
French origin. Add crushed black peppercorns and finely minced shallots to red-wine vinegar. Serve with raw oysters or shellfish.

milk gravy (see country gravy)

mint sauce
British origin. Mix sugar and vinegar. Salt and pepper to taste. Bring to a boil. Infuse mint. Process. Serve chilled.

mojo rojo [MOH-HOH roh-hoh]
Spanish origin (Canary Islands). Caribbean variations. Blend Jerez vinegar, oil, chopped garlic, paprika, cilantro, parsley, sweet red peppers, and toasted almonds. Salt and pepper to taste. Add water to achieve sauce consistency. Chill.

mojo verde [MOH-HOH vair-day]
Spanish origin (Canary Islands). Caribbean variations. Blend Jerez vinegar, oil, chopped garlic, cilantro, parsley, sweet green peppers, toasted almonds, and cumin. Salt and pepper to taste. Add water to achieve sauce consistency. Chill.

mole [MOH-lay]
Sauce. Mexican origin. Many variations. Sauté dried chili peppers, onions, and garlic. Add Mexican spices. (If desired, add bread crumbs.) Process and make a thick paste. Dilute with water or stock.

mole negro [MOH-lay NAY-groh]
Black sauce. Mexican origin. Stir-fry onions, ancho, guajillo, and cascabel chilies. Reserve. Toast cloves, peppercorns, thyme, cumin, sesame seeds, and peanuts. Blend. Grill tortilla until dry and crispy. Blend tomatoes and tomatillos and bring to a boil. Reserve. Mix together chilies, toasted spices and nuts, grilled tortilla, and tomatoes. Process. Simmer. Add Mexican dark chocolate and melt. Add salt, pepper, and sugar to taste.

mole poblano [MOH-lay poh-BLAH-noh]
Puebla sauce. Mexican origin. Sauté ancho, mulato, and pasilla chilies, then grind. Sauté sesame seeds, chopped almonds, peanuts, corn tortilla, bread crumbs, cloves, tomatoes, diced onions, garlic, oregano, and anise seeds, then grind. Mix together and add cinnamon, salt, Mexican chocolate, and sugar. Dilute with water or stock as needed. (If desired, add garnish of toasted sesame seeds.)

mole rojo [MOH-lay ROH-hoh]
Red sauce. Mexican origin. Grind stir-fried onions, garlic, and pasilla and ancho chilies into a smooth paste. Add water as needed. Cook a few minutes. Add stir-fried ground nuts and sesame seeds. Add water as needed. Salt and pepper to taste.

mole verde [MOH-lay VAIR-day]
Green sauce. Mexican origin. Grind tomatillos, lettuce leaves or other greens, garlic, onions, cilantro, cumin, and chilies into a smooth paste. Add water as needed. Cook a few minutes. Add stir-fried ground pumpkin seeds and peanuts. Add water as needed. Salt and pepper to taste.

Mornay [mor-NAY]
French origin. Melt cheese in béchamel. Monter au beurre.

mousseline [moos-LEEN]
French origin. Start with hollandaise and then fold in whipped cream.

moutarde [MOO-tard]
French origin. Start with hollandaise and add Dijon mustard.

Nantua [nan-TWAH]
French origin. Sauté mirepoix and crawfish. Flambé with cognac. Add white wine and fish stock. Add tomato concassée, fish velouté, salt, and pepper. Simmer for 1 hour or until sauce consistency.

Newburg sauce
Sauté lobster meat, salt, cayenne pepper, and shells. Flambé with cognac. Reserve lobster meat. Add cream and fish stock. Simmer 30 minutes. Pass through chinois. Monter au beurre. Add lobster meat back into the sauce.

noir [NWAR] **butter**
French origin. Cook butter until the color is black. (If desired, add vinegar.)

noisette [nwah-ZET] **butter**
French origin. Cook butter until the color of hazelnuts.

Normande [nor-MAHND] **sauce**
French origin. Start with fish velouté. Add mushroom cooking juices. (If desired, add oyster or mussel juices.) Add cream and reduce. Monter au beurre. Salt and pepper to taste. (If desired, add mussels and sautéed mushrooms.)

nuoc cham [noo-ahk CHAHM]
Vietnamese origin. Bring vinegar and sugar to a boil. Cool. Mix in chopped garlic, chopped chili peppers, lime juice, and fish sauce. Serve at room temperature.

orange sauce (see gastrique)

Oxford (see Cumberland)

pan drippings (see au jus)

parsley sauce
British origin. Sauté bay leaves, parsley stalks, mace, cracked peppercorns, and chopped onions in butter. Add flour to make a white roux. Add milk and proceed as with béchamel. Pass through chinois. Add fresh chopped parsley and finish with lemon juice. Salt and pepper to taste.

peanut sauce
Thai origin. Many variations. Process toasted peanuts. Sauté chopped shallots, ginger, and garlic. Add soy sauce, brown sugar, coriander, and cumin. Add water and simmer. Add peanuts and lemon juice. Blend.

Périgourdine [pair-ee-gour-DEEN]
French origin. Start with demi-glace. Add foie gras and process until smooth. Add sliced truffles. Salt and pepper to taste.

Périgueux [pair-ee-GOUH]
French origin (Périgueux). Start with demi-glace. Add Madeira, truffle essence, and chopped truffles. Salt and pepper to taste.

pesto alla Calabrese [ka-lah-BRAY-zay]
Italian origin (Calabria). Process skinless grilled bell peppers, garlic, toasted pine nuts, Parmigiano-Reggiano, and basil. Whisk in olive oil. Salt and pepper to taste.

pesto alla Genoese [jen-oh-EEZ]
Italian origin (Genoa). Process garlic, toasted pine nuts, Parmigiano-Reggiano, and basil. Whisk in olive oil. Salt and pepper to taste.

pesto alla Genovese [jen-oh-VEEZ] (see pesto alla Genoese)

pesto alla Siciliana [SEE-cheel-yah-nah]
Italian origin (Sicily). Process garlic, skinless and seeded tomatoes, Parmigiano-Reggiano, and basil. Whisk in olive oil. Salt and pepper to taste.

pesto alla Trapanese [TRA-pah-NAY-zay]
Italian origin (Trapani). Process garlic, basil, and toasted almonds. Whisk in olive oil. Add chopped, seedless, skinless tomatoes. Salt and pepper to taste.

pesto rosso [ROH soh]
Italian origin. Process sun-dried tomatoes, extra-virgin olive oil, black olives, garlic, fines herbes, salt, and pepper.

picalilli relish [ROH soh]
American origin (Southern). Salt (dry-brine) diced bell peppers, onions, and cucumbers. Bring sugar, vinegar, and pickling spices to a boil. (If desired, add chili peppers.) Add rinsed vegetables. Bring to a boil again. Can or reserve relish.

pico de gallo [PEE-koh day GA-yoh]
Mexican origin. Brunoise seeded tomatoes, onions, and serrano chilies. Add chopped fresh cilantro. Salt to taste.

piquante [pee-KAHNT]
French origin. Reduce chopped shallots in ½ white wine and ½ vinegar. Add demi-glace and simmer. Finish with chopped gherkins, chopped parsley, chervil, and tarragon. Salt and pepper to taste.

pistou [PEES-too]
French origin. Process garlic, Parmigiano-Reggiano, and basil leaves until slightly coarse. Whisk in olive oil. Add chopped, peeled, seeded tomatoes. Salt and pepper to taste.

poivrade [pwahv-RAHD]
French origin. Sauté mirepoix with parsley stalks, thyme, bay leaves, coarse peppercorns, and bits of game meat. Deglaze with vinegar. Reduce. Add demi-glace. Simmer. Pass through chinois. Salt and pepper to taste.

poor man's gravy (see red-eye gravy)

Port sauce
Reduce Port with chopped shallots and thyme. (If desired, add orange juice and zest.) Add demi-glace. Add cayenne pepper. Salt and pepper to taste.

poulette [POO-let]
French origin. Start with velouté (preferably chicken). Add mushroom cooking juices. Finish with lemon juice and chopped parsley. Salt and pepper to taste.

Provençal [proh-vahn-SAHL]
French origin. Start with tomato concassée. Add chopped garlic and parsley. Add white wine and simmer 30 minutes.

puttanesca [poo-tah-NEZ-kah]
Italian origin. Start with tomato sauce. Add anchovies, capers, garlic, chili peppers, and black olives. Simmer 30 minutes. Salt and pepper to taste.

raita [rah-EE-tah]
Indian origin. Process mint leaves, cilantro, cumin, toasted caraway seeds, and cayenne pepper. (If desired, add cucumbers.) Add yogurt and process. Salt and pepper to taste. Serve chilled.

ranch dressing; ranch dipping sauce
American origin. Equal parts mayonnaise, sour cream, and buttermilk. Add garlic powder, dill, and Worcestershire. Salt and pepper to taste. Emulsify.

ravigote [rah-vee-GOT]
French origin. Reduce half white wine and half vinegar. Add velouté. Whisk in shallot butter. Finish with chopped fines herbes. Salt and pepper to taste.

recado [re-KAH-doh]
Mexican origin. Bring water and achiote seeds to a boil for 2 hours and steep. Sauté garlic and onions. Process with achiote seeds, Mexican oregano, allspice, chile powder, cider vinegar, and lime juice.

red-eye gravy
American origin (Southern). Many variations. Roast country ham. Reserve cooking fat. Deglaze pan with black coffee. Variations: Add mustard or ketchup (Alabama). Use red wine instead of coffee (Mississippi). Serve with country ham or beef (Louisiana).

red ham gravy (see red-eye gravy)

red sauce (see tomato sauce)

red wine sauce
Reduce chopped shallots with red wine. Add stock as desired. Monter au beurre. Salt and pepper to taste.

red wine vinaigrette [vee-nuh-GRET]
Mix red wine vinegar, sugar, lemon juice, salt, pepper, Worcestershire, dry English mustard, chopped garlic, olive oil, and vegetable oil.

rémoulade [ray-muh-LAHD]
French origin. Start with mayonnaise. Add Dijon mustard, chopped capers, gherkins, parsley, and tarragon. Finish with lemon juice. Salt and pepper to taste. Serve cold.

Robert [roh-BAIR]
French origin. Sauté chopped onions until translucent. Add white wine, vinegar, and cracked peppercorns. Reduce. Add demi-glace. Add Dijon mustard.

roebuck
   English origin. Sauté diced onions and ham. Add vinegar and
   bouquet garni. Reduce. Add demi-glace. Add Port and gooseberry
   jelly. (If desired, add cayenne pepper.) Salt and pepper to taste.

romesco [roh-MES-koh]
   Spanish origin (Catalonia). Process roasted, skinless tomatoes, roasted
   garlic, toasted almonds, hazelnuts, and seared dried chilies. Salt and
   pepper to taste. Add olive oil slowly as if making mayonnaise. Finish
   with Jerez vinegar.

rouille [roo-EE]
   French origin (Southern). Crush garlic in mortar or food processor
   with saffron and red chili peppers. Add mustard. (If desired, add
   cooked potato.) Salt and pepper to taste. Add 1 egg yolk. Slowly
   add 1 cup of olive oil. Emulsify. Finish with lemon juice and
   cayenne pepper.

rumescu (see romesco)

Russian dressing
   American origin. Mix mayonnaise, ketchup, Worcestershire,
   horseradish, pimientos, onions, and chives. Salt and pepper to taste.

salsa alla marinara (see marinara)

salsa de tomate rojo [day toh-MAH-tay ROH-hoh] (see tomato salsa)
   Red tomato salsa.

salsa de tomate verde [day toh-MAH-tay VAIR-day]
   Green tomato salsa. Proceed as with tomato salsa but use green tomatoes.

salsa marinara (see marinara)

salsa ranchera [ran-CHEH-rah]
   Rancher's sauce. Mexican origin. Purée peeled tomatoes, onions, garlic,
   and blanched serrano chilies to make a red, uncooked tomato sauce.
   Simmer for a few minutes. Salt and pepper to taste.

sambal [SAM-bahl]
   Southeast Asian origin. Regional variations. Similar to chutney.
   Process aromatic element such as garlic, ginger, or fruit with a spicy
   element such as chili peppers. Blend with sugar and vinegar. Serve
   with main course.

sausage gravy
Sauté country sausage. Reserve. Make a roux with the pan drippings. Add milk like a béchamel. Add sautéed sausage. Simmer. Salt and pepper to taste.

sawmill gravy (see country gravy)

soubise [soo-BEEZ]
French origin. Sauté chopped onions until translucent. Add béchamel. Simmer 30 minutes. Process with hand blender. Salt and pepper to taste.

soy dipping sauce
Many variations. Mix soy sauce, water, rice vinegar, sugar, and chopped scallions. Serve at room temperature.

steak sauce
Many variations. Mix ketchup, chopped onions, garlic, Worcestershire, lemon juice, white vinegar, soy sauce, brown sugar, mustard, and water. Simmer. Process. Chill.

supreme sauce
Combine equal parts velouté, chicken or veal stock, and heavy cream. Reduce by two-thirds. Monter au beurre.

sweet and sour
Chinese-American origin. Bring rice vinegar, brown sugar, ketchup, and soy sauce to a boil. Thicken with cornstarch. (If desired, add pineapple juice and Chinese spices.)

tabasco-style sauce
Boil tabasco peppers and garlic in white vinegar until soft. Add sugar, salt, and horseradish. Process. Steep 2 weeks in refrigerator.

tandoori sauce
Indian origin. Mix yogurt, ginger paste, garlic paste, cumin, garam masala, and saffron. Chill.

tartare; tartar
Start with mayonnaise. Add cooked egg yolks, chopped shallots, and cayenne pepper. Salt and pepper to taste. Serve cold.

Thermidor [THER-mi-dohr]
French origin. Start with Bercy sauce. Add mustard and Mornay sauce.

Thousand Island dressing
American origin. Mix mayonnaise, ketchup, hard-boiled eggs, diced gherkins, horseradish, and Worcestershire. (If desired, add chopped green olives, peppers, and onions.) Salt and pepper to taste.

tomato concassée [kon-kah-SAY]
French origin. Sauté diced onions. Add skinless, seedless, diced tomatoes. Add garlic, bay leaf, and sugar for acidity correction. Salt and pepper to taste. Reduce until slightly dry.

tomato salsa
Mexican origin. Mix diced tomatoes, chopped garlic, Anaheim green chilies, scallions, jalapeños, fresh cilantro, olive oil, and lime juice. Salt and pepper to taste. Serve chilled.

tomato sauce
Sauté mirepoix and garlic. (If desired, add bacon or pancetta until slightly brown.) Add tomato concentrate. (If desired, add roux.) Deglaze with white or red wine. Add peeled and seeded ripe tomatoes. Reduce. Add sugar for acidity correction. Add herbs such as bay leaf, thyme, rosemary, oregano, and basil. Salt and pepper to taste. Simmer for hours. (If desired, process until smooth.)

Tyrolienne [tee-rohl-YEN]
Blend mayonnaise with tomato paste or reduced tomato concassée. Add Worcestershire, cayenne pepper, and chopped fine herbs such as parsley and chervil.

tzatziki [tsat-ZEE-kee]
Greek origin. Process mint leaves, dill, cucumber, cayenne pepper, garlic, lemon juice, and olive oil. Add yogurt and process. Salt and pepper to taste. Serve chilled.

velouté [vuh-loo-TAY]
French origin. Start with clear chicken stock. (If desired, use fish or veal stock.) Thicken with blonde roux.

verte [VAIRT]
Blanch spinach, watercress, tarragon, chervil, and parsley or other fines herbes. Process. Add mayonnaise. (If desired, add cayenne pepper and lemon juice.) Salt and pepper to taste.

Victoria
Start with allemande sauce. Add white wine and mushrooms. Simmer. Whisk in lobster coral and monter au beurre. (If desired, add tomato concentrate or reduced tomato concassée.) Salt and pepper to taste.

vinaigrette [vee-nuh-GRET]
French origin. Mix 3 parts oil and 1 part vinegar. Add salt and pepper. (If desired, add herbs, spices, shallots, Dijon mustard, or garlic.)

Vincent [vehn-SAHN]
French origin. Mix 50% sauce verte and 50% sauce tartare.

vinegar sauce
American origin (Southern). Many variations. Simmer apple cider vinegar and red pepper flakes. Salt and pepper to taste. (If desired, add brown sugar, honey, lemon juice, Worcestershire, or ketchup.) Chill.

white barbecue sauce
American origin (Alabama). Mix mayonnaise, cider vinegar, lemon juice, and cayenne pepper. Salt and pepper to taste. (If desired, add sugar, corn syrup, and horseradish.)

white gravy (see country gravy)

white sauce (see béchamel)

white wine sauce
Start with fish or chicken stock. Add white wine. Reduce greatly. Monter au beurre. Salt and pepper to taste.

zingara [zin-GAH-rah]
Sauté shallots. Deglaze with white wine. Add demi-glace and brunoise of cooked mushrooms, ham, tongue, and truffles. Add fair amount of cayenne pepper. Salt and pepper to taste.

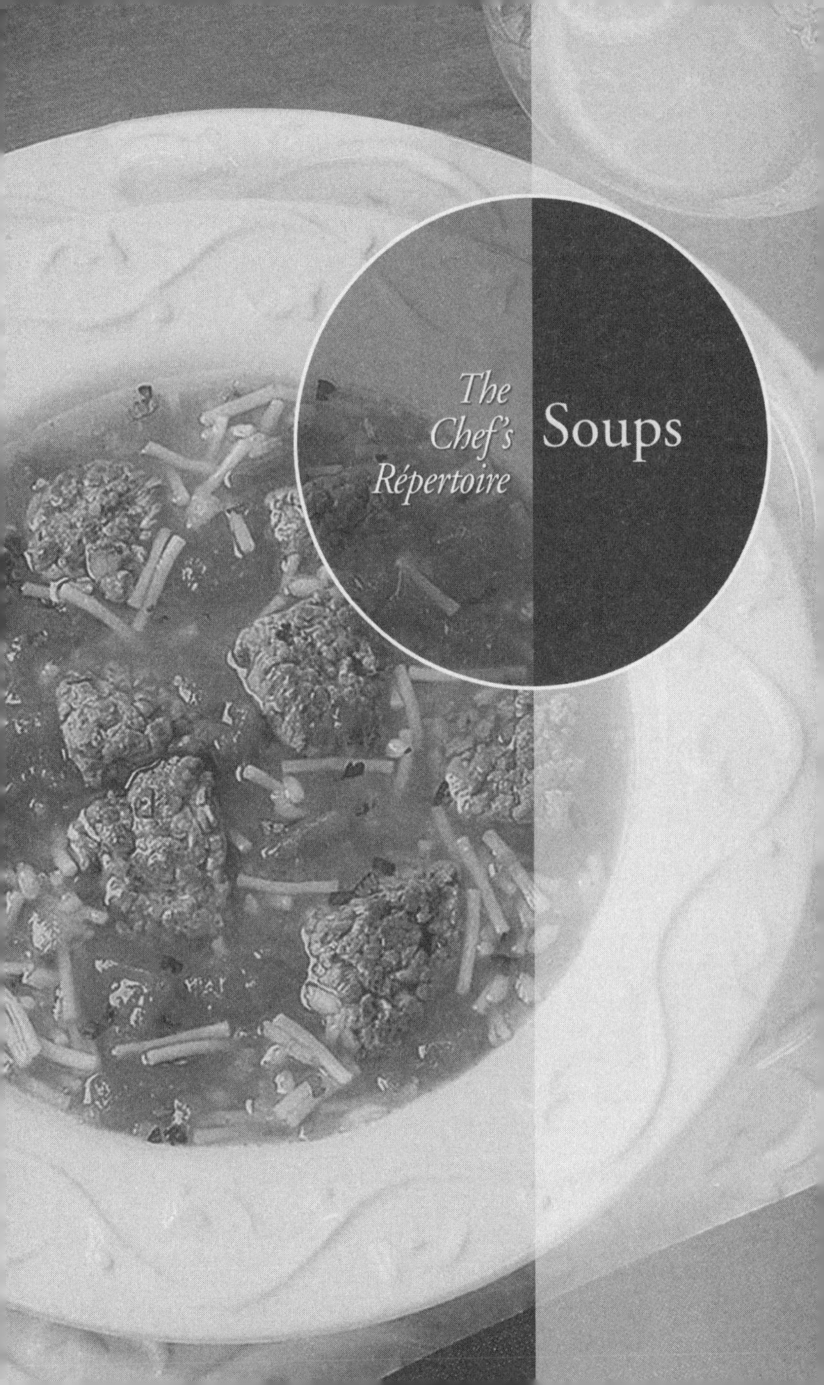
The Chef's Répertoire
Soups

acquacotta [ak-wa-KOH-tah]
Cooked water. Italian origin (Tuscany). Sauté onions and celery. Wilt greens. Add tomatoes, chili peppers, water, chopped parsley, salt, and pepper. Simmer. Poach eggs and reserve. To assemble, place toasted rustic bread slice in a soup plate and top with poached egg. Pour soup and sprinkle with Parmigiano-Reggiano.

aigo boulido [IGH-goh boo-lee-DOH]
Boiled garlic. French origin (Provence). Boil water with garlic cloves, fresh sage, salt, and pepper. Process. Poach eggs in soup and reserve. Thicken with egg yolks. Do not boil. To assemble, place toasted rustic bread in a soup plate and top with poached egg. Pour soup and drizzle with extra-virgin olive oil.

avgolemono [ahv-goh-LEM-uh-noh]
Greek origin. Cook rice in chicken stock. Add milk and thicken with egg yolks. Do not boil. Add butter, chopped parsley, lemon juice, and grated lemon peel. Salt and pepper to taste. (If desired, add shredded chicken.)

Bergen fish soup
Norwegian origin. Poach carrots, parsnips, leeks, and cold-water fish such as cod or halibut in a fish stock. Thicken with egg yolks. Do not boil. Salt and pepper to taste.

Bergen's fiskesuppe [FIS-kuh SOO-peh] (see Bergen fish soup)

billi bi [BILL-ee bee]
French origin. Cook mussels with white wine, fresh parsley, and shallots "à la marinière." Thicken cooking juices with cream and egg yolks. Add shelled mussels. Salt and pepper to taste.

Boerenkaas Soep [BORE-en-kahss SOO-puh] (see Dutch Farmer's cheese soup)

borscht [BORSHT]
Russian origin. Sauté cabbage and onions. Add beef broth, fresh beets, vinegar, salt, and pepper. Simmer. Process until smooth.

Brunswick stew
American origin. Sauté onions and bacon. Sear beef and chicken. Add cooked ham and water. Salt and pepper to taste. Simmer. Add tomatoes, potatoes, and corn. Simmer. Finish with okra, lima beans, and green beans.

caldo Tlalpeño [KAHL-doh tla-PAYN-yoh]
Mexican origin. Sauté garlic, onions, carrots, and poblano and chipotle peppers. Add chicken and chicken stock. Simmer until chicken is cooked. Shred the chicken and return to soup. Add rice. Simmer until rice is tender. To serve, add lime and cilantro. (If desired, add radish and avocado garnish.)

caldo verde [KAHL-doh VAIR-day]
Green broth. Portuguese origin. Sauté onions and garlic. Add chicken stock and potatoes. Simmer until thickened, but still chunky. Add chorizo. Add kale or collard greens. Salt and pepper to taste.

callaloo [KA-lah-loo]
Caribbean origin. Sauté bacon, diced ham, onions, garlic, and scallions. Add spinach or Swiss chard and chicken stock. Simmer. Add crab meat, grouper, okra, and coconut milk. Salt and pepper to taste. Simmer to finish the soup.

cassola [ka-SOH-lah]
Mediterranean origin. Sardinian and Catalonian variations. Similar to bouillabaisse. Cook mussels with white wine. Shell mussels. Sauté onions and basil. Add squid and brown. Add sun-dried tomatoes, garlic, and chili peppers. Add cooking juices from mussels, peeled and seeded tomatoes, fish stock, shrimp, and Mediterranean fish filets. Salt and pepper to taste. Finish with fresh parsley. Serve with toasted bread.

cataplana [ka-tah-PLAH-nah]
Portuguese origin. Quickly steam clams in a cataplana or covered Dutch oven with fish stock, port, red and green bell peppers, onions, zucchini, squash, linguica or chorizo sausage, tomatoes, salt, and pepper. Poach white fish such as cod or monkfish in the soup. Finish with lemon juice and chopped parsley.

cawl [KAH-wul]
Welsh origin. Regional variations. Sear diced lamb. Add stock and simmer for one hour. Add root vegetables and cabbage. Finish cooking. Top with chopped parsley.

cazuela [ka-zway-lah]
Spanish/South American origin. Many regional variations. Traditionally cooked in earthenware. Braise beef, chicken, or pork with potatoes and pumpkin. (If desired, add cooked rice, noodles, green beans, celery, carrots, or corn.)

chicken soup cockaigne [kah-kayn]

American origin. Boil chicken with vegetables such as carrots, parsnips, celery, onions, and leeks. Add herbs, garlic, and mace. Salt and pepper to taste. Simmer until chicken is tender. Shred chicken and return to soup.

chili, Boston

American origin (Boston). Sauté onions, bell peppers, and garlic. Add beef and pork. Add tomatoes, chili powder, jalapeño peppers, and cumin. Salt and pepper to taste. Deglaze with red wine and add beans. Serve with cheese, chopped cilantro, red onions, and sour cream on the side.

chorba [CHOR-buh]

North African origin (Mahgreb). Regional variations. Simmer lamb meat, onions, tomatoes, carrots, celery, potatoes, turnips, and chickpeas. Add spices such as cumin, saffron, and turmeric. (If desired, add vermicelli.) Finish with chopped cilantro and mint.

cioppino [chuh-PEE-noh]

Italian origin. Similar to bouillabaisse. Prepare a base sauce by sautéing garlic, onions, celery, bell peppers, and Mediterranean herbs. Add vinegar, tabasco, Worcestershire, and tomato sauce. Simmer. Poach fish such as halibut and snapper and shellfish such as scallops, shrimp, crab, clams, and mussels in the base sauce.

congee [KAHN-jee]

Chinese origin. Asian variations. Start with sushi rice. Add water and simmer until soup becomes silky. Add soy sauce and pepper to taste. (If desired, add ginger, garlic, greens, tofu, and beans.)

consommé [KON-soh-may]

French origin. Roast bones (veal, beef, or chicken) or lobster shells until slightly brown. Cover with cold water. Add mirepoix and cloves. Salt and pepper to taste. Add lean meat. Simmer 3 to 5 hours. Clarify. When consommé is chilled, add ground meat and egg whites. Mix well and quickly bring to a boil. Pass through chinois and a coffee filter for a crystal-clear consommé.

consommé brunoise [KON-soh-may BROON-wahz]

French origin. Proceed as with consommé. Add carrots, leeks, and celery brunoise. Finish cooking vegetables until al dente.

corn chowder
American origin. Sauté bacon. Add onions and celery. (If desired, add corn cobs without kernels.) Add milk and potatoes. Simmer 20 minutes. Remove corn cobs. Add corn. Salt and pepper to taste. Finish simmering the chowder. Process until half-smooth.

country captain
American origin (Southern). Sear chicken with curry, ginger, and chili peppers. Reserve. Sauté onions, bell peppers, and garlic. Add chicken stock, tomatoes, and apples. Add chicken and simmer.

dashi [DAH-shee]
Japanese origin. Many variations. Similar to vegetable stock. Bring water to a boil. Add konbu seaweed and shaved katsubushi. Turn off heat and infuse.

Dutch Farmer's cheese soup
Dutch-American origin. Sauté bacon and onions. Add carrots, cauliflower, and celery root. Add chicken stock and simmer. To serve, top with bread, then gouda cheese, and broil until golden. Serve immediately.

encebollado [en-se-boh-YAH-doh]
Ecuadorian origin. Make a refrito with onions, tomatoes, cumin, chili powder, garlic, and salt. Add water. Poach tuna. Add boiled yucca. Serve with lime and avocado garnish.

fanesca [fah-NES-kah]
Ecuadorian origin. Desalt cod. Make a refrito with onions, garlic, achiote, cumin, and oregano. Add cooked rice, zucchini, and butternut squash. Process until smooth. Add cabbage, fava beans, peas, corn, lima and cannellini beans, roasted peanuts, milk, and cod. Simmer. Add queso fresco or cream cheese. Serve with sides of hard-boiled eggs, pickled onions, fried plantains, slices of queso fresco, hot sauce, and cheese empanadas.

French onion
French origin. Caramelize onions. Add roux. Add beef broth, peppercorns, salt, pepper, and cloves. Simmer. Place in bowls. Top with crostini or dry bread, and Emmental, Gruyère, or Swiss. Brown in oven.

Soups

garbure [gar-BYUR]
French origin (Southwest). Precook cabbage in duck fat. Start soup with salt pork, precooked cabbage, onions, carrots, turnips, white beans, and herbs. Salt and pepper to taste. Simmer for 2 hours. To finish, add confit d'oie (goose legs in rendered fat).

gazpacho [gahz-PAH-choh]
Spanish origin (Andalusia). Skin fresh ripe tomatoes. Purée. Garnish with brunoise sweet peppers, onions, celery, cucumbers, garlic, cayenne pepper, and olive oil. (If desired, add vinegar or lemon juice for acidity.) Marinate 24 to 48 hours. Serve chilled.

goulash [GOO-lahsh]
Hungarian origin. Sauté onions. Sauté beef with paprika. Add stock and simmer. Add halved potatoes, tomatoes, and green peppers. Simmer. Serve with dumplings and sour cream.

harira [hah-REE-rah]
Moroccan origin. Sauté onions with Moroccan herbs such as turmeric, cumin, ginger, saffron, and paprika. Sauté diced lamb and tomatoes. Deglaze and add water. Bring to simmer. Add parboiled chickpeas, then lentils. Add rice or noodles in the last 15 minutes. Infuse with fresh coriander and parsley. Finish with lemon juice.

hotch potch
Scottish origin. Simmer lamb neck with salt and pepper. When almost cooked, add onions, carrots, and turnips. Simmer. Add peas and cauliflower.

jook (see congee)

Lady Curzon soup
British origin. Make a turtle soup. Add curry, cream, and sherry. Simmer.

lobster bisque [bisk]
French origin. Sauté mirepoix with lobster shells. Flambé with cognac. Deglaze with white wine. Add lobster stock, peeled and seeded tomatoes, rice, paprika, and cayenne. Salt and pepper to taste. Simmer. Finish with cream. Garnish with lobster meat. (If desired, add lemon juice and fresh tarragon.)

locro [LOH-croh]
South American origin. Ecuadorian, Argentinian, and Peruvian variations. Sauté onions with chorizo. Add tomatoes, navy beans, and dry herbs. Simmer until beans are cooked. Add corn, salt, and pepper.

Louisiana court-bouillon [kort BOOL-yahn]
American origin (Louisiana). Make a brown roux. Add green peppers, celery, onions, garlic, thyme, tomatoes, fish stock, and chili peppers. Simmer. Add long-grain rice, Worcestershire, and white fish such as haddock or snapper. Salt and pepper to taste.

Manhattan clam chowder
American origin (Manhattan). Proceed as with New England clam chowder but add tomatoes instead of milk or cream.

matzah [MAHT-suh] **ball soup** (see matzo ball soup)

matzo [MAHT-suh] **ball soup; matzoh ball soup**
Jewish origin. Make a soup with chicken, onions, carrots, and celery. Salt and pepper to taste. To make matzo balls, mix chopped parsley, eggs, matzo meal, and chicken fat. Poach in chicken stock. Add matzo balls to soup.

minestrone [mi-ne-STROH-nay]
Italian origin. Dice seasonal vegetables and beans. Cover with cold water. Simmer. Add pasta or rice at the end of the cooking process. Rectify with salt and pepper. (If desired, add grated Parmigiano-Reggiano, olive oil drizzle, and infused chopped basil.)

miso [MEE-soh] **soup**
Japanese origin. Bring dashi stock to a simmer. Add sliced mushrooms. Then add miso diluted with soy sauce. Add tofu. Heat, but remove before boiling. Infuse with chopped scallions.

mock turtle soup
American origin. Sear diced veal meat or oxtails. Add mirepoix and dried herbs such as oregano and thyme. Add tomato purée and chicken or beef stock. Thicken with brown roux. Simmer. Salt and pepper to taste. Finish with lemon juice, tabasco, chopped parsley, and chopped hard-boiled eggs.

Soups

mulligatawny [muhl-ig-guh-TAW-nee]
British-Indian origin. Sauté onions. Add carrots, parsnip, potato, rice, and lamb. Add curry paste, stock, salt, and pepper. Simmer. Purée slightly, leaving chunks.

Nantucket scallop chowder
American origin (Nantucket). Sauté bacon and onions. Add herbs, fish or clam stock, white wine, and potatoes. Simmer. Add cream and sautéed scallops. Add salt and pepper.

New England clam chowder
American origin (New England). Sauté bacon. Add onions and sauté. Add diced potatoes and clam stock. Simmer until potatoes are tender. Add chopped clams and milk or heavy cream. Salt and pepper to taste. Simmer. Finish with chopped parsley. (If desired, add lemon juice.)

oyster bisque [bisk]
American origin (New England). Proceed as with oyster stew. Thicken with egg yolks.

oyster stew
American origin (New England). Sauté onions until transparent. And milk and cream. Salt and pepper to taste. Simmer. Add shucked oysters and chopped parsley.

Pacific Northwest salmon chowder
American origin (Northwest). Sauté bacon and onions with dry herbs. Add potatoes and fish stock. Simmer until slightly thickened. Salt and pepper to taste. Add salmon chunks. Simmer until cooked. Finish with cream.

parmentier [pahr-MAHN-tyay] (see potage parmentier)

pasta e fagioli [PAH-stah eh faj-YOH-lee]
Pasta and beans. Italian origin. Sauté onions, pancetta, and garlic. Add cooked kidney or white beans, peeled and seeded tomatoes, broth, and Mediterranean herbs. Simmer. Add al dente macaroni. Salt and pepper to taste. Sprinkle with Parmigiano-Reggiano and drizzle with extra-virgin olive oil.

paysanne [PAY-zahn]
French origin. Paysanne-cut carrots, potatoes, leeks, and turnips. Simmer in chicken stock until vegetables are done. Salt and pepper to taste. (If desired, add bacon or oxtail for flavor.)

peanut soup
American origin (Georgia). Sauté onions and celery. Add flour to make a roux. (If desired, add potatoes and corn.) Add chicken stock. Simmer and thicken. Add peanut butter, cream, and cayenne. Salt and pepper to taste. Garnish with peanuts.

Pennsylvania Dutch chicken corn soup
American origin (Pennsylvania). Boil chicken quarters in water or stock. Simmer until cooked through. Shred the meat. Add corn kernels and egg noodles to the broth. (If desired, add dumplings.) Add shredded meat and chopped hard-boiled eggs. Finish with chopped parsley. Salt and pepper to taste.

pho bo [fah bow]
Vietnamese origin. Poach onion, ginger, and star anise in beef stock. Add salt and sugar. Cook flat rice noodles. Shock noodles in ice water. To assemble, place thin stripes of raw beef, scallions, and cilantro in individual bowls. Add noodles and broth. Serve with bean sprouts, basil, cilantro, and chili peppers.

pistou [PEES-too] **soup** (see soupe au pistou)

posole [poh-SOH-leh]
Mexican origin (Pacific coast). Boil pork shoulder or butt with garlic. Simmer until tender. Add hominy or posole corn, jalapeño chili peppers, cumin, oregano, salt, and pepper. Simmer. Serve with side of shredded cabbage, radishes, onions, and lime.

potage parmentier [poh-TAHZH pahr-MAHN-tyay]
French origin. Sauté leeks (white portion only). Add chicken stock and potatoes. Simmer. Process until smooth. Salt and pepper to taste.

potage paysanne [poh-TAHZH PAY-zahn] (see paysanne)

potage Saint-Germain [poh-TAHZH san-zher-MEHN]
French origin. Sauté onions. Add green peas, bacon, and chicken stock. Simmer. Salt and pepper to taste. Process. Finish with cream. (If desired, add croutons, fresh peas, and chervil.)

Soups

potée [POH-tay]

French origin. Regional variations. Poach ham in broth and onion piqué with clove. Poach thick-sliced bacon and local sausages. Poach turned potatoes, turned carrots, turned turnips, leeks, and cabbage in broth. (If desired, add beans such as navy beans.) Reserve. Serve with side of coarse sea salt, Dijon mustard, and gherkins.

pozole [poh-ZOH-leh] (see posole)

Rhode Island clam chowder

Make Manhattan clam chowder and add chorizo and red pepper flakes.

ropa vieja [ROH-pah VYAY-hah]

Cuban origin. Boil flank steak with onions, green peppers, tomatoes, garlic, and cumin. Salt and pepper to taste. Simmer until meat is tender. Shred meat and return to soup.

Scotch broth

Scottish origin. Sauté ground lamb and reserve. Sauté onions and carrots. Wilt kale or cabbage. Mix vegetable ingredients. Salt and pepper to taste. Add barley, bay leaf, and chicken stock. Simmer. Add cooked lamb and malt vinegar. Serve immediately. Variation: Boil cubed lamb shoulder. Add barley, leeks, carrots, and celery. Salt and pepper to taste. Simmer until lamb is tender.

Senate

American origin. Parboil navy beans. Sauté onions, celery, garlic, potatoes, and ham. Add parboiled beans. Process until creamy but still chunky. Salt and pepper to taste. Finish with chopped parsley.

she-crab soup

American origin (Charleston). Sauté onions and celery. Add flour to make a white roux. Add fish stock. Add Worcestershire, cayenne pepper, and milk. Simmer. Add female crab meat. (If desired, add roe.) Finish with dry sherry. Salt and pepper to taste.

snapper soup (see turtle soup)

soupe à l'oignon [soop ah LAHN-yohn] (see French onion soup)

soupe au pistou [soop oh PEES-too]
  French origin (Provence). Proceed as with minestrone using the
  following vegetables: leeks, onions, carrots, celery, zucchini, green
  beans, tomatoes, cannellini beans, broad beans, and potatoes.
  (If desired, add angel hair pasta.) Salt and pepper to taste. Serve
  with pistou sauce, grated parmesan, and extra-virgin olive oil as
  accompaniments. Variation: Mix pistou, grated parmesan, and extra-
  virgin olive oil into the soup prior to serving.

split pea soup
  German origin. Sauté bacon until crispy. Sauté onions and carrots.
  Add chicken stock, split peas, and ham hocks. Salt and pepper to
  taste. Simmer.

stracciatella [strah-chee-ah-TEL-ah]
  Italian origin. Simmer chicken stock. Whisk in eggs, Parmigiano-
  Reggiano, bread crumbs, chopped parsley, chopped garlic, and
  nutmeg. Whisk until eggs are coagulated.

tarbiya [tahr-BEE-yuh] (see avgolemono)
  Arabic origin.

terbiye [ter-BEE-yuh] (see avgolemono)
  Turkish origin.

turtle soup
  American origin. Sear diced turtle meat. Add mirepoix and dried
  herbs such as oregano and thyme. Deglaze with sherry. Add tomato
  purée and chicken or beef stock. Thicken with brown roux. Simmer.
  Salt and pepper to taste. Finish with lemon juice, tabasco, chopped
  parsley, and chopped hard-boiled eggs.

vichyssoise [VEE-shee-swahz]
  French-American origin. Sauté leeks and onions. Add potatoes, salt,
  and pepper. Cover with chicken stock. Simmer. Finish with cream.
  Process until smooth. Serve hot or cold.

Soups

Soups

Appetizers

accra
Carribean origin. Make a batter with 1 cup flour, ¼ cup milk, 1 egg, salt, and ¾ teaspoon baking powder. Cut bite-sized portions of desalted salted cod. Dip cod in batter. Deep-fry.

affettato [af-eh-TAH-toh]
Italian origin. A platter of Italian cold cuts.

anchoïade; anchoiade; anchoyade [ahn-shwah-YAHD]
French origin (Provence). Rinse and desalt anchovies. Process anchovies, garlic, basil, black olives, capers, bread crumbs, and olive oil into a paste. Serve on toast or with raw vegetables.

angels on horseback
British origin. Wrap each oyster with a slice of bacon and secure with toothpicks. (If desired, add anchovy paste.) Serve on individual toasts.

antipasto [an-tee-PAS-toh]
Italian origin. Assemble a platter of Italian cold cuts. Garnish with marinated peppers, olives, and cheeses.

arepas [ah-RAY-pas]
South American origin. Regional variations. Similar to flatbread. Mix 1½ cups arepa flour, 1 tablespoon sugar, salt, and 1 cup grated cheese such as mozzarella. Add 3 cups hot milk and ¼ cup butter. Let cool. Shape into small cakes. Sear until golden and cooked through. (If desired, add stuffing or toppings.)

assiette anglaise [ah-SYET AHN-glez] (see ploughman's lunch)

baba ghanoush; baba ghannouj [bah-bah gah-NOOSH]
Middle Eastern origin. Roast whole eggplant. Purée pulp. Add tahini, olive oil, lemon juice, and garlic. (If desired, add chopped mint.) Serve with pita or flatbread.

bagna cauda [BAN-yah KOW-dah]
Italian origin. Process olive oil, anchovies, garlic, and butter. Adjust seasoning with salt and pepper. Serve fondue style, with bite-sized fresh vegetables or crusty bread.

blini [BLEE-nee]
Russian origin. Similar to small pancakes. Mix together ¼ cup warm water, 1¼ teaspoons dry yeast, and 1½ tablespoons sugar. Let yeast activate. Add ½ cup flour, ½ cup buckwheat flour, ¼ teaspoon salt, 1 cup milk, ¼ cup butter, and 2 eggs. Let yeast activate and the volume of dough increase. When dough is ready, sauté blini. (If desired, add filling ingredients such as grated potatoes, apples, or raisins.)

blintz [BLINTS]
Jewish origin. Many variations. Similar to crêpes. Mix together 1½ cup flour, 2 cups milk (use water for pareve), 3 tablespoons butter, 2 tablespoons sugar, 2 eggs, ½ teaspoon baking powder, and salt to taste. Let dough rest. Sauté blintzes. Fill with cheese, potatoes, fruit, or applesauce.

bocconcini [boh-kohn-CHEE-nee]
Italian origin. Marinate mozzarella in garlic, Italian herbs and spices, and infused olive oil. Cut into small bites.

brandade [brahn-DAHD]
French origin (Provence). Italian and Spanish variations. Desalt salted cod. Process cooked cod with warm milk and olive oil. Salt and pepper to taste. (If desired, add garlic or mashed potatoes.) Serve hot or cold.

bresaola [brez-ah-OH-lah]
Italian origin. Defat leg of beef. Dry-cure in salt and spices such as juniper, cinnamon, or nutmeg. (If desired, marinate with red wine, mirepoix, salt, and herbs such as rosemary, thyme, bay leaves, peppercorn, and juniper.) Dry-age 1 to 3 months. Slice thin and serve as antipasto.

bruschetta [broo-SKEH-tah]
Italian origin. Similar to crostini. Grill bread and drizzle with olive oil. Top with ingredient combinations such as diced tomatoes, garlic, and basil.

Buffalo wings
American origin (Buffalo, New York). Many variations. Toss wings in flour. Deep fry at 375°F. When fully cooked, toss wings in melted butter, red-wine vinegar, and hot red-pepper sauce. Serve with celery sticks and blue cheese dressing.

Appetizers

Cajun popcorn
American origin (Louisiana). Make a batter with 1 cup flour,
1 teaspoon sugar, 1 teaspoon salt, ½ teaspoon thyme, ½ teaspoon
Cajun spices, 1½ cups milk, and 2 eggs. Dip crawfish in batter. Toss
in cornmeal. Deep fry at 375°F.

canapé [KA-nah-PAY]
French origin. Use a toasted, fried, grilled, or plain sliced baguette
or a shaped white bread as a base. Add a spread of compound butter,
flavored cream cheese, or aïoli. Add a main ingredient such as steamed
shrimp, figs, seared duck breast, or raw tuna. Garnish with chervil,
chives, other fines herbes, caviar, or lemon zest.

caponata [kap-oh-NAH-tah]
Italian origin (Sicily). Local variations. Steam or sauté eggplant. Sauté
onions and celery. Add tomato concassée or pulp. Add eggplant, black
olives, and capers. (If desired, add vinegar and sugar.) Let thicken.
Salt and pepper to taste. Serve chilled.

carpaccio [kahr-PAH-chee-oh]
Italian origin. Thinly slice (paper-thin) beef, salmon, tuna, or other
raw protein. Pound between parchment paper. Top with lemon juice,
herbs and a drizzle of olive oil. Salt and pepper to taste.

ceviche [seh-VEE-chay]
Latin American origin. Many regional variations. Dice raw grouper,
sea bass, Mahi Mahi, shrimp, or scallops. Marinate with lime or
lemon juice, chopped onions, chilies, garlic, salt, cayenne pepper,
parsley or cilantro, and tomatoes.

chalupa [chah-LOO-pah]
Mexican origin. Use a base of cornmeal dough (masa de mais) and
shape into small boats. Deep-fry. Fill with a combination of salsa,
marinated pork, and shredded beef or chicken. (If desired, add
vegetables or cheese.)

charmoula [CHAHR-moo-lah]
North African origin (Mahgreb). Regional variations. Process toasted
cumin, garlic, cilantro, Italian parsley, lemon juice, paprika, and
cayenne pepper into a paste. Monter with olive oil. Salt and pepper to
taste. Chill. Use as sauce, marinade, or dip.

Appetizers

chaud-froid [shoh-FWAH]
French origin. Section appetizer-sized pieces of chicken or fish. Adequately cook, then chill. Glaze with aspic and decorate with fines herbes and cut vegetable decorations. Garnish with fines herbes.

chicharrón [chee-chah-ROHN]
Mexican origin. Deep-fry pork skin twice, once in 325°F oil, then again in 375°F oil, making it balloon into honeycombed puffs.

chicken fingers
Make a batter with ½ cup milk, 1 egg, 1 tablespoon of vegetable oil, and 1 tablespoon of water. Make a dry coating with ½ cup bread crumbs, ½ cup cornmeal, ½ cup flour, and salt and pepper to taste. Dip chicken tenders into batter, then into dry coating. Deep-fry at 375°F.

chimichanga [chee-mee-CHAN-gah]
Mexican origin. Southwestern and Tex-Mex variations. Similar to a deep-fried burrito. Start with corn tortilla. Fill with ground beef, chicken, cheese, beans, rice, or any mixture of these ingredients. (If desired, add onions, chilies, cilantro, tomatoes, garlic, or potatoes.) Fold tortilla like an envelope. Secure with toothpicks. Deep-fry.

chirashi [chee-RAH-shee]
Japanese origin. Cook sushi rice. Prepare different cuts of sashimi such as tuna, salmon, swordfish, and shrimp. Prepare different cuts of vegetables such as cucumbers, daikon, radishes, and snap peas. Make a thin egg crêpe (kinshi tamago), then roll it and julienne. To assemble, put the chilled sushi rice in a Japanese bowl. Scatter the sashimi, egg crêpe, and vegetables on top of the rice. Add wasabi, salmon roe (ikura) and julienned kizammi nori.

chow-chow; chowchow relish
Dry-brine sliced cucumbers or shredded cabbage and reserve. Bring sugar, vinegar, and dry mustard to a boil. Thicken sauce and reserve. Steam diced green tomatoes, green bell peppers, peas, cauliflower, and onions. Add rinsed cucumbers or cabbage. Add sauce. (If desired, preserve relish for later use.)

cicharón [tzee-chah-ROHN] (see chicharrón)

clams casino

American origin. Process scallions and fresh parsley. Add butter and soften. Add lemon juice and salt to taste. Place clams on the half shell. Place 1 teaspoon of mixture on top of each clam. Top with bacon bits. Broil.

clams oreganata

Italian origin. Open raw clams and stuff the half shell with a mixture of bread crumbs, oregano, parsley, mint, salt, pepper, and olive oil. Bake at 375°F.

coca

Spanish origin (Catalonia). Make dough by dissolving 1 oz fresh yeast in 1 cup of water. Add 1 cup butter or lard and 4 tablespoons olive oil. Add flour. Let rest, then roll dough. Sauté sliced peppers, tomatoes, garlic, paprika, and chopped parsley. Top the dough with the vegetable mix. Bake at 375°F. Serve warm, chilled, or at room temperature.

Cornish pasty [PAS-tee]

British origin (Cornwall). Many variations. Prepare a flaky pastry or puff pastry dough. Roll out in a circle. Garnish the inside with cooked steak, potatoes, onions, rutabagas, or other savory fillings. (If desired, add a savory filling at one end of the pastry and a sweet filling at the other end.) Fold over and crimp the top. Egg-wash. Bake until golden.

coulibiac [koo-lee-BYAHK]

Russian origin. French adaptation. Many variations. Prepare a brioche dough. Roll out into a rectangle. Garnish one lengthwise half of the rectangle with layers of prepared items such as salmon, cooked rice, sautéed mushrooms, or hard-boiled eggs. Fold dough over and overlap edges. Roll over and tuck to make a chimney. Egg-wash. Bake until golden.

crab rangoon

American origin. Process scallions. Add crab meat and cream cheese. (If desired, add ginger, garlic, soy sauce, and Worcestershire.) Fold into won ton wrappers. Deep-fry.

creton [KRAY-ton]
Canadian origin (Québec). Similar to rillette. Slowly braise ground pork butt in water and milk with onions and spices such as cinnamon, allspice, nutmeg, and bay leaves. (If desired, add garlic.) Drain. Reserve fat. Add cooking juices for moisture. Force into a bowl. Top with fat. Chill and reserve. Serve at room temperature.

crisps
Grate cheese such as Parmigiano-Reggiano or Manchego on a silicone mat. (If desired, add herbs and spices.) Bake at 350°F until golden. Let cool. Remove from silicone mat and break into pieces.

croque monsieur [krohk muh-SYER]
French origin. Toast white bread. Top with cooked ham, thick béchamel, and grated cheese. Broil. Serve hot.

croquettes [kroh-KET]
French origin. Many variations. Similar to fritters. Make a base with mashed potatoes, minced meat, fish, or vegetables and spices and herbs. Shape into bite-sized cylinders or footballs. (If desired, dip in egg batter.) Roll in bread crumbs. Deep-fry.

crostini [kroh-STEE-nee]
Little toasts. Italian origin. Use a toasted or grilled sliced baguette, ciabatta, or shaped white bread as a base. Drizzle with olive oil. (If desired, top with a combination of ingredients such as tomato, mozzarella, and basil.) Serve with soups, salads, or dips.

crudités [kroo-dee-TAY]
French origin. Cut raw vegetables such as carrots, celery, bell peppers, broccoli, and cauliflower. Serve with vinaigrette or dipping sauce.

deviled crab
Cuban origin. Make a dough with soaked white bread, bread crumbs, and paprika. To make crab meat filling, sauté chopped onions and chopped green peppers. Add Cuban enchilada sauce or a tomato-based hot sauce. Add crab meat. To assemble, press 3 parts dough and 1 part crab mixture and roll into a football shape. Roll into flour. Dip in egg batter. Deep-fry.

deviled eggs
Peel hard-boiled eggs, cut in half, and remove yolk. Add mayonnaise, Dijon mustard, salt and pepper, cayenne pepper or paprika. (If desired, add parsley to the yolks.) Blend. Pipe mixture back into each egg half. Serve chilled or at room temperature.

devils on horseback (see pigs in blankets)

dolma [dohl-MAH]; **dolmades** [dohl-MAH-dez]
Middle Eastern origin. Many variations. Blanch grape leaves. Stuff with a mixture of cooked ground lamb, rice, onions, and parsley. (If desired, add pine nuts and raisins.) Serve warm with yogurt-based sauce.

doner-kebab; doner-kabob [DUH-ner kuh-BOB]
Middle Eastern origin. Skewer thin slices of lamb, beef, chicken or pork, superposed with ground lamb, beef, chicken, or pork on a vertical rotisserie. Cook meat. Serve on pita bread. (If desired, add tomatoes, onions, lettuce, and yogurt-based sauce.)

dumplings
Pieces of dough (sometimes filled) that are boiled, pan-fried, deep-fried, or steamed. Alternate forms include pot stickers, ravioli, jiaozi, gyoza, won ton, pierogi, vareniki, and mandu.

egg roll
Asian origin. Many regional variations. Similar to spring roll but with a thicker, crunchier skin. Stir-fry chicken, pork, beef, shrimp, or crab and add raw or quickly stir-fried vegetables such as mushrooms, bean sprouts, scallions, and julienne carrots. Season with soy sauce, ginger, cilantro, oyster sauce, rice-wine vinegar, sesame oil, and Asian spices or condiments. Place filling on top of two sheets of wheat-based egg roll wrappers. Wrap in a diamond shape, wet edges, roll over, tuck, roll again and seal. Dip in egg wash. Deep-fry.

empanada [em-pah-NAH-dah]; **empañada** [em-pah-NYAH-dah]
Iberian origin. Many variations. Make dough from 3 cups flour, 1 teaspoon salt, ½ cup water, 1 egg, 1 egg white, 1 teaspoon vinegar, and 3 tablespoons shortening. Make filling from cooked ground beef, chilies, green olives, diced onions, and cheese. Fill pastry, seal, and deep-fry.

escabèche [es-kah-BESH]
Spanish origin. International variations. Fry fish. Marinate overnight in vinegar (or half vinegar and half white wine) with chopped onions, tomatoes, parsley, carrots, celery, garlic, fennel seeds, salt, whole peppercorns, and herbs such as oregano, rosemary, thyme, and bay leaves. (If desired, add capers.) Served chilled.

falafel; felafel [fah-LAH-fuhl]
Middle Eastern origin. Process uncooked chick peas or fava beans with parsley, cilantro, salt, chili peppers, garlic, and cumin until coarse. Add baking powder and flour. Form small balls. Fry in hot oil.

farinata [fah-ree-NAH-tah]
Italian origin (Liguria). Similar to pizza, but paper-thin. Make dough with 1 cup chick pea flour, 2 cups water, salt, and olive oil. Roll dough until thin. Add toppings. Bake at 550°F.

frico [FREE-koh]
Italian origin. Similar to crisps. Sauté thin pancakes of grated Parmigiano-Reggiano or Montasio cheese. Season with paprika. Serve soft or crunchy, depending on type of cheese.

fritters (see croquettes)

gnocchi [NYOH-kee]
Italian origin. Many variations. Similar to small potato dumplings. Boil 3 lb of potatoes. Pass through mill, add 2 cups flour, 1 egg, and salt to taste. Shape into balls or concave disks. Poach like pasta. Serve with olive oil or bake with tomato-based sauce, cheese, pesto, or béchamel-based sauce.

gougère [goo-ZHAIR]
French origin (Burgundy). Similar to choux pastry. Use 1 cup water, 4 tablespoons butter, and ¾ teaspoon salt. Add 1½ cups flour. Mix into homogenous paste. Dry until paste is semi-dry and pulls away from sides of pan. Remove from heat. Add 4 eggs, one at a time. Add grated Gruyère and pepper. Pipe desired size rings or disks onto silicone mat. Bake at 375°F until golden brown and dry.

gravlax [GRAHV-lahks]
Swedish origin. Start with whole raw salmon filets. Debone. Sprinkle with dill. (If desired, add crushed peppercorns.) Cover completely with salt and sugar mixture for 24 to 48 hours. Rinse. Marinate in olive oil for 36 to 48 hours. Serve cold. Slice à la minute.

Appetizers

grissini [gri-SEE-nee]
Breadsticks. Italian origin. Mix together 1 teaspoon active yeast,
¼ cup warm water, and ½ tablespoon sugar. Let yeast activate for a
few minutes. Add 1¼ cups semolina flour, 1½ cups Italian "00" or all-
purpose flour, salt, and olive oil. Beat dough until soft and elastic. Let
rise for 1½ hours at room temperature. Roll dough into thin breadsticks.
Bake at 350°F.

guacamole [gwah-kah-MOH-lay]
Avocado sauce. Mexican origin. Many variations. Mash a ripe avocado.
Add lime juice and finely chopped onions, tomatoes, jalapeño
peppers, and fresh cilantro. Salt and pepper to taste.

guotie [gaw-AH-tee] (see jiaozi)

gyoza [GYO-zah]
Japanese origin. Regional variations. Roll dough very thin. Make filling
of minced pork, garlic, cabbage, and chives. Boil, pan-fry, or deep-fry
dumplings. Serve with soy-based and rice-vinegar dipping sauce.

hummus [HOOM-uhs]
Middle Eastern origin. Regional variations. Process cooked or canned
chick peas, tahini, lemon juice, salt, and cayenne pepper. Monter with
olive oil. (If desired, add herbs such as garlic or another main ingredient.)

jiaozi [jee-AH-oh-zee]
Dumpling. Chinese origin. Regional variations. Roll dough
moderately thin. Make a filling of pork, lamb, beef, chicken, fish or
shrimp, chopped vegetables, and herbs. Boil, steam, or fry. Served
with soy sauce-based dipping sauce.

kapunata
Maltese origin. Similar to ratatouille. Sauté peeled, diced eggplants,
onions, peppers, tomatoes, and celery. Add garlic and Mediterranean
herbs. Salt and pepper to taste. Simmer and reduce. Add black olives
and capers. (If desired, add vinegar.) Serve chilled or warm.

kibbeh [KIH-beh]; **kibbi; kibbe** [KIH-bee]
Middle Eastern origin (Syria). Many regional variations. Mix bulgur,
chopped onions, and ground lamb. (If desired, add spices and herbs
such as mint.) Shape into meatballs or torpedoes. Deep-fry. Variation:
Shape in a sheet pan and bake.

kilted sausages (see pigs in blankets)

kuku [koo-koo]
Iranian origin. Similar to frittata. Beat eggs with garlic, fresh herbs, fenugreek, and Persian spices. (If desired, add flour, baking powder, salt, and pepper.) Bake.

labneh; labaneh [LAB-neh]
Middle Eastern origin. Mix yogurt and salt to taste. Drain in coffee filter at room temperature for 24 hours. Unmold and refrigerate for 12 hours. Shape into balls with chopped mint and paprika. Marinate in olive oil.

latke [LAHT-kuh]
Jewish origin. Similar to potato pancakes. Prepare a mixture of 2 lb grated potatoes, 1 lb grated onions, ½ cup flour, and 3 eggs. Salt and pepper to taste. Sauté pancakes and finish in oven.

Liptauer [LIP-tow-er] **cheese**
Hungarian origin (Liptauer). Process cream cheese (or ewe's milk) with paprika. Add minced onions and capers. (If desired, add garlic.) Serve with black bread.

liver mousse (see liver pâté)

liver pâté [pah-TAY]
French origin. Sauté onions and garlic. Add herbs. Salt and pepper to taste. Add chicken livers, white wine, and butter. Simmer. Process until smooth. Chill.

maki [MAH-kee]
Japanese origin. Layer sushi rice with nori, raw fish strips and/or vegetable strips. Roll with bamboo sheet. Slice the roll to desired size. Serve with Japanese soy sauce, wasabi, and pickled ginger.

mandu [MAN-doo]
Korean origin. Boiled or steamed meat- or vegetable-filled dumplings served in soup.

moussaka; mousaka [moo-SAH-kah]
Greek origin. Many regional variations, notably in the Middle East, the Balkans, and Turkey. Sauté eggplant slices in olive oil. Layer with cooked ground lamb, onions, and tomatoes. Top with béchamel sauce. (If desired, add cheese.) Bake.

Appetizers

mousse, liver (see pâté)

muhammara [moo-hahm-RAH]
Syrian origin. Similar to hummus. Process roasted, skinless red bell peppers, garlic, walnuts, coarse bread crumbs, lemon juice, cumin, and cayenne pepper until puréed. (If desired, add pomegranate syrup.) Monter with olive oil. Salt and pepper to taste. Garnish with mint leaves.

nachos [NAH-chohs]
Mexican origin. Sprinkle tortilla chips with grated cheddar or Monterey Jack and mild green chili peppers. Broil. Top with sour cream and cilantro.

negimaki [NAH-gee-MAH-kee]
Japanese origin. Pound out thin slices of steak. Roll steak around flash-blanched scallions. Secure with toothpicks. Instant-marinate in teriyaki sauce and grill. Slice and serve.

nigiri [nee-GEE-ree]
Japanese origin. Many variations. Make a small oval-shaped bowl of sushi rice. Top with slice of raw fish. Serve with Japanese soy sauce, wasabi, and pickled ginger.

oysters Rockefeller
American origin (Louisiana). Many variations. Sauté shallots. Wilt spinach or a selection of fresh herbs such as tarragon, chervil, Italian parsley, and green onions. Chop finely. Add Pernod, fresh butter, black pepper to taste, and bread crumbs. (If desired, add grated Parmigiano-Reggiano.) Top oysters on the half shell with sauce. Broil. Serve immediately.

paillasson [PIGH-uh-sohn]
French origin. Similar to potato pancakes. Grate potatoes. Salt and pepper to taste. Shape into small pancakes. Sauté and finish in oven.

pan a la Catalana [PAN ah lah kat-ah-LAN-ah] (see pan con tomate)

pan con tomate [pan kohn toh-MAH-tay]
Bread with tomato. Spanish origin (Catalonia). Toast bread such as a baguette. Rub with fresh garlic. Cut tomato in half and place on toasted bread. Drizzle with extra-virgin olive oil and salt. Serve immediately.

pasty [PAS-tee] (see Cornish pasty)

pâté [pah-TAY]
French origin. Many variations. Use ¼ lean pork, chicken, or veal, ½ country sausage, and ¼ ground bacon. (If desired, add chicken livers, vegetables such as asparagus, scallions, or spinach, or nuts such as pistachios or walnuts.) Salt and pepper to taste. Add cayenne pepper to taste. Add cognac or liquor. Press in a terrine. Bake in a bain-marie. Serve chilled.

picada [pee-KAH-dah]
Spanish origin (Catalonia). Many variations. Process garlic, parsley, nuts such as almonds, hazelnuts, pine nuts or walnuts, stale bread, and olive oil into a thick paste. (If desired, add hard-boiled egg yolks and chicken livers.) Dilute with pan juice. Add to Catalan sauce dishes for flavor enhancement.

pico de gallo [PEE-koh day GA-yoh]
Mexican origin. Brunoise seeded tomatoes, onions, and Serrano chilies. Add chopped fresh cilantro. Salt to taste.

pierogi [pee-ROH-gee]
Slavic origin. Polish, Russian, and Ukrainian variations. Similar to dumplings or ravioli. Make dough with 3 cups flour, 1 whole egg, 1 egg yolk, salt, and ¾ cup warm water. Knead. Let rest. Flatten. Cut to appropriate size. Fill with various fillings such as cheese and potatoes, mushroom, sauerkraut or cabbage. Top with bacon bits and sautéed onions.

pigs in blankets
Roll franks in puff pastry brushed with Dijon mustard. Section into bite-sized pieces. Brush with egg yolk. Bake.

pissaladière [pee-sah-lah-DYAIR]
French origin (Provence). Make dough with 1⅓ cups flour, 2 teaspoons baking powder, 3⅓ tablespoons cold unsalted butter, ½ cup milk, and salt. Top the flattened dough with caramelized onions, anchovies, niçoise olives, a drizzle of olive oil, and herbes de Provence. (If desired, add sautéed red peppers.) Bake.

ploughman's lunch
British origin. Combine cold items such as cheese, cold cuts, bread, pickled onions, gherkins, mixed greens, hard-boiled eggs, cooked beets, and pâté on an individual plate.

pot stickers
Chinese origin. Regional variations. Similar to jiaozi. Pan-fried.

pupusa [poo-POO-suh]
Salvadoran origin. Similar to flatbread. Make dough with 2 cups cornmeal flour and 1 cup water. Shape small cakes. Sear until golden and cooked through. Serve. (If desired, add stuffing or toppings.)

quesadilla [KAY-sah-DEE-yah]
Mexican origin. Fill 2 tortillas with cheese such as Monterey Jack. Heat on griddle until cheese is melted. (If desired, add stuffing or toppings.) Serve immediately.

quiche [KEESH]
French origin. Roll out flaky pastry dough into tart pan. Alternatively use puff pastry. Fill tart shell with sautéed vegetables, meat, or other fillings. Make a custard using 1 egg per cup of cream, half and half, or milk. Salt and pepper to taste. Add nutmeg. Pour custard over fillings. Bake at 375°F until custard is set and bottom of tart is dry.

quiche Lorraine [KEESH loh-REN]
French origin. Proceed as with quiche. Fill with sautéed diced bacon before adding custard.

raita [rah-EE-tah]
Indian origin. Process mint leaves, cilantro, cumin, toasted caraway seeds, and cayenne pepper. (If desired, add cucumbers.) Add yogurt and process. Salt and pepper to taste. Serve chilled.

rarakor
Swedish origin. Similar to latkes. Prepare a mixture of 2 lb grated potatoes, ½ cup flour, fresh chives, and salt and pepper to taste. Sauté and finish in oven.

ratatouille [ra-tuh-TOO-ee]
French origin (Provence). Many variations. Dice eggplant, zucchini, red peppers, and onions. Sauté each vegetable separately. Gather in one pan. Add chopped, peeled, and seeded tomatoes. Add garlic and herbes de Provence. Salt and pepper to taste. Simmer 20 minutes.

ravioli [ra-VYOH-lee]
Italian origin. Make pasta dough. Roll sheet paper-thin. Egg-wash half of the surface. Make filling of ricotta, beef, spinach, sausage, or any combination of these items. Pipe dollops of filling 2 inches apart on half the sheet. Fold the other half sheet on top of the fillings. Press out air pockets and seal in fillings. Cut into squares. Dust with flour and reserve. Boil like fresh pasta. Serve with tomato-based sauce, grated cheese, or pesto.

rillette [REE-yett]
French origin. Slowly braise pork shoulder, pork belly, and fatback with herbs, garlic, and carrots. Drain. Reserve fat. Shred meat. Add cooking juices for moisture. Force into a bowl. Top with fat. Chill and reserve. Serve at room temperature.

roschti [ROOSH-tee] (see rösti)

rösti [ROO-stee]
Swiss origin. Similar to potato pancakes. Prepare a mixture of grated potatoes. Salt and pepper to taste. (If desired, add bacon, onions, cheese, or herbs.) Sauté and finish in oven.

rumaki [roo-MAH-kee]
American origin. Marinate chicken livers and water chestnuts in soy sauce, ginger, dry sherry, and sugar. Wrap one piece of liver and one chestnut with a bacon slice. Roast at 375°F until crisp.

samfaina [sam-FIGH-nah]
Spanish origin (Catalonia). Many variations. Dice eggplant, red peppers, and onions. Sauté vegetables separately. Gather in one pan. Add chopped, peeled and seeded tomatoes. Add garlic and herbes de Provence. Salt and pepper to taste. Simmer 20 minutes.

samosas [sah-MOH-sahs]
Indian origin. Make filling with mashed potatoes, sautéed onions, peas, garlic, cilantro, and chili peppers. Brush phyllo sheets with melted butter. Cut phyllo into strips. Add filling to one end of each strip. Fold in triangles like a flag. Brush with melted butter. Bake.

Saratoga chips
Similar to potato chips. Slice peeled potatoes paper thin. Soak in water. Drain and dry potatoes. Deep-fry at 380°F. Cook until golden. Drain on paper towels. Salt to taste.

Appetizers

sashimi [sah-SHEE-mee]
Japanese origin. Slice fresh fish such as tuna or salmon. Serve raw with Japanese soy sauce, wasabi, and pickled ginger.

satay; saté [sah-TAY]
Southeast Asian origin. Many regional variations. Similar to kebobs. Marinate beef or chicken strips with coarse peanut butter, soy sauce, coconut milk, ground cumin, ground coriander, curry paste, lime juice, sesame seeds, and sesame oil. Skewer and grill meat. Serve with or without dipping sauce.

seviche [seh-VEE-chay](see ceviche)

shawarma [shah-WAHR-mah] (see doner-kebab)

shish-kebab; shish kabob [SHISH kuh-bob]
Turkish origin. Skewer meat cubes such as lamb, pork, chicken, or beef with vegetables such as bell peppers and onions. Marinate with spices and herbs. Grill and serve.

slider
American origin. Mini-sandwich.

sofregit [so-FRAH-zhit]
Spanish origin (Catalonia). Caramelize onions. Add peeled, chopped, ripe tomatoes. (If desired, add sugar for acidity correction.) Simmer and reduce.

soufflé [soo-FLAY]
French origin. Make a flavorful, thick béchamel base. Add a combination of goat cheese or blue cheese and meat, fish, crawfish, or chicken livers, vegetable purée of beets or peas, and herbs such as tarragon, thyme, and chives.

souvlaki [soo-VLAH-kee]; **souvlakia** [soo-VLAH-kee-uh]
Greek origin. Marinate diced pork or chicken in lemon juice, olive oil, and Mediterranean herbs overnight. Skewer and grill. Salt and pepper to taste.

spanakopita [span-uh-KOH-pih-tuh]
Greek origin. Mix feta and Kefalotiri (or other Greek cheese) with eggs, dill, salt, and pepper. Wrap in triangles of phyllo dough or make a pie.

spring roll
   Asian origin. Many regional variations. Stir-fry chicken, pork, beef, shrimp, or crab and add raw or quickly stir-fried vegetables such as mushrooms, bean sprouts, scallions, and julienned carrots. Season with soy sauce, ginger, cilantro, oyster sauce, rice-wine vinegar, sesame oil, and Asian spices or condiments. Place filling on two sheets of rice paper. Wrap in a diamond shape, wet edges, roll over, tuck, roll again, and seal. Deep-fry.

strudel [STROO-duhl]
   German origin. Many variations. Lay out several layers of phyllo dough and brush with butter. Wrap desired mixture of mushroom béchamel, walnuts, apples, cheese, chicken, and wild rice. Bake in 400°F oven until golden brown.

sushi [SOO-shee] **rice**
   Japanese origin. Wash 2 cups of short-grain rice three times. Add 2 cups of water. Bring to a boil, then simmer 15 minutes. Let rest 10 minutes. Heat up 2 tablespoons of rice vinegar with 2 tablespoons of sugar. Add the vinegar-sugar mixture to the rice. Cool.

tamales [tuh-MAH-lays]
   Mexican origin. Many regional variations. Soak dried corn husks. Make a cornmeal dough (masa de mais) and place inside rehydrated corn husks. (If desired, add filling such as refried beans, fish, shredded chicken, or stewed beef.) Wrap by folding and tying the corn husk. Steam. Serve hot.

tapenade [TA-puh-nahd]
   French origin (Provence). Spanish and Italian variations. Process black or green olives with garlic into a paste. (If desired, add anchovies and capers.) Monter with olive oil.

tarama [tah-rah-MAH] (see taramosalata)

taramosalata [tah-rah-MAH-sah-LAH-tah]
   Greek origin. Turkish and Bulgarian variations. Process plain or smoked cod roe, white bread, and lemon juice. Monter with olive oil. Salt and pepper to taste. Chill.

tartine [tahr-TEEN]
   French origin. Similar to crostini. Use plain or toasted baguette slices or other bread. Top with jam, pâté, butter, or smoked salmon.

terrine [tuh-REEN] (see pâté)

Appetizers

tortellini [tor-te-LEE-nee]
Italian origin. Make pasta dough. Roll sheet paper-thin. Cut into 4-inch rounds. Make filling from ricotta, beef, spinach, sausage, or any combination of these items. Pipe filling into each round. Egg-wash around the filling. Fold each round in half to cover filling. Then fold dough back around your finger, sticking corners together. Dust with flour and reserve. Boil like fresh pasta. Serve with tomato-based sauce, grated cheese, or pesto.

tortilla de patatas [tohr-TEE-yuh day pah-TAH-tahs]
Spanish origin. Blanch and sauté potatoes in abundant olive oil. (If desired, add onions.) Mix in beaten eggs, cover, and cook very slowly to coagulate the eggs. Tortilla must be thick, not too brown, and evenly cooked. Serve warm or cold.

tyropita [TEER-uh-peet-uh]
Greek origin. Mix feta and Kefalograviera (or other Greek cheese) with eggs, dill, salt, and pepper. Wrap in phyllo dough triangles or make a pie.

vareniki [vah-ren-NE-kee]
Ukrainian origin. Regional variations. Similar to pierogi. Mix 6 cups flour, 2 eggs, 2 cups water, and salt to taste. Knead. Let rest. Flatten. Cut to appropriate size. Fill with various fillings such as potatoes and mushrooms, cabbage, sauerkraut, fish, meat, or berries.

vitello tonnato [vee-TEL-oh tuh-NAH-toh]
Italian origin. Poach lean roast veal with mirepoix until meat is tender. Reserve and chill. Slice thin. Make a blended sauce with canned tuna, anchovies, capers, extra-virgin olive oil, and lemon juice. Fold in mayonnaise. Spread tuna sauce on veal slices and marinate overnight. Serve chilled.

vol-au-vent [vawl-oh-VAHN]
French origin. Make two equal rounds from a puff pastry sheet. Cut a smaller round inside one of the rounds and remove the excess. Brush both rounds with egg yolk. Stack the smaller round on top of the larger round. Brush with egg yolk. Bake until golden (dry on the outside and moist on the inside). Fill with hot or cold filling such as béchamel, financière, ragu, or fish mousse.

Appetizers

wiener winks (see pigs in blankets)

won ton; won-ton [WAHN tahn]
Chinese origin. Regional variations. Roll dough moderately thin and fill with minced pork and herbs. Form right triangle or purse-shaped dumplings. Boil, pan-fry, or deep-fry.

*The
Chef's
Répertoire* Eggs

à la coque [AH LAH kok] (see soft-boiled)
In its shell.

au plat [oh plah] (see pan-fried)

baked
Break egg into a buttered ramekin. Salt and pepper to taste. Drizzle with cream. Bake in a bain-marie at 350°F until egg is set and yolk thickens but is still runny.

basted
Proceed as with pan-fried eggs but baste the top of the eggs with hot butter. Cover pan between bastings. Salt and pepper to taste. Serve warm.

Beatrice
Halve English muffins. Toast. Top with sautéed tomato slices. Sauté eggs sunny-side up. Place eggs on top of tomato slices. Sauce with a shallot and red wine vinegar reduction. Sprinkle with fresh parsley or tarragon. Serve warm.

Benedict
Toast a slice of biscuit or halved English muffin. Top with ham or Canadian bacon, poached egg, and hollandaise. Serve warm.

bibimbap [be-beem-bop]
Korean origin. Boil rice. Wilt spinach. Sauté bean sprouts. Sauté julienned zucchini. Stir-fry kosari. Sauté shitake mushrooms. Sauté ground beef and season with soy sauce, garlic, sugar, and peppers. Sauté julienned carrots. Prepare egg sunny-side up. To assemble, place rice in the middle of a large platter and display vegetables and meat around it. Place egg on top. Drizzle with sesame oil and chili oil. Serve immediately.

Blackstone
Sear lightly floured tomato slices. Top with poached eggs, then diced fried bacon and hollandaise.

Carême [KAH-raym]
French origin. Scramble eggs with diced foie gras, cooked chicken meat, and truffles.

coddled (see poached)

Denver omelet (see Western omelet)

deviled eggs
Peel hard-boiled eggs, cut in half, and remove yolk. Add mayonnaise, Dijon mustard, salt and pepper, cayenne pepper or paprika. (If desired, add parsley to the yolks.) Blend. Pipe mixture back into each egg half. Serve chilled or at room temperature.

egg in-a-hole
Cookie-cut a hole into a slice of sandwich bread. Sauté bread slice in hot butter. Add egg in the hole. Sauté until egg whites are coagulated. Flip over and finish cooking. Salt and pepper to taste. Serve warm.

eggnog
Make a custard by combining 1 cup milk, 1 cup heavy cream, 4 egg yolks, ⅓ cup sugar, nutmeg, and cinnamon. Cook over low heat to thicken. Do not heat over 175°F. Add brandy or rum. Chill. Serve cold.

en cocotte [ahn koh-KAHT] (see baked)
In an oven-proof dish.

flamiche [flah-MEESH]
French origin. Proceed as with quiche. Fill with sautéed leeks.

Florentine
Toast a slice of biscuit or English muffin. Top with wilted spinach and poached egg. Coat with hollandaise or Mornay sauce. Serve warm.

foo yong [foo YUHNG]
Chinese-American origin. Stir-fry scallions, onions, and bean sprouts. Add garlic. Add soy sauce, cooked ham, salt, and pepper. (If needed, thicken with cornstarch.) Mix with eggs and make thin omelets. Layer omelets on serving dish. Serve with sauce made of soy sauce, dry sherry, and cornstarch.

fried (see pan-fried)

frittata [fri-TAH-tuh]
Italian origin. Unfolded omelet garnished with goat cheese, roasted garlic, fines herbes, tomatoes, spinach, or other leafy greens as desired. Beat whole eggs with other ingredients. Coagulate eggs over moderate high heat. Do not fold. Serve as flat-sided, oval shape.

Hangtown fry
American origin (California). Dip shucked oysters into flour, then egg batter, then bread crumbs. Sauté oysters. Add beaten eggs and make a flat omelet. Serve warm.

hard-boiled
Plunge eggs in boiling water with a drizzle of vinegar. No salt. Boil 10 minutes.

huevos rancheros [WAY-voss ran-CHEH-ros]
Farmer's eggs. Mexican origin. Prepare tomato-chipotle salsa. Cook eggs sunny-side up. Serve on warm tortillas. Sauce with warm tomato-chipotle salsa around the eggs. (If desired, top with queso fresco and chopped cilantro.) Serve with refried beans.

matzo brei [MAHT-suh brigh]
Jewish origin. Make a mix of matzo flour and water. Add beaten eggs. Salt and pepper to taste. Proceed as with omelet.

meurette [mer-RET]
French origin. Poach eggs in red wine. Reserve eggs. Reduce wine with carrots, onions, and celery brunoise. Add demi-glace. Serve poached egg on sourdough baguette toasts. Garnish with sautéed bacon, mushrooms, and shallots. Nappé with red wine sauce.

mollet [MAW-lay]
French origin. Plunge in boiling water with a drizzle of vinegar. No salt. Boil for 5 minutes. Shock in ice water. Serve on salads.

omelet; omelette [AHM-let]
Beat eggs. Season with salt and pepper. Pour into nonstick sauté pan. Stir briskly with fork. When eggs are semicoagulated to coagulated, roll into football shape or leave as is. (If desired, fill rolled omelet with garnish.) Serve warm.

omelet Napoletana
Italian origin. Cook spaghetti and sauté in butter. Add beaten eggs, milk, nutmeg, ham, mozzarella, salt, and pepper. Proceed as with omelet.

over-easy
Proceed as with pan-fried eggs but flip the egg over once the white is coagulated. Cook a few seconds without browning. Salt and pepper to taste. Serve warm.

over-hard
Proceed as with eggs over-easy but cook until yolk has coagulated. Salt and pepper to taste. Serve warm.

pan-fried
Break egg into a ramekin. Sauté in warm butter until white is coagulated but yolk is still runny. Salt and pepper to taste. Serve warm.

poached
Break the egg in a ramekin. Plunge egg in boiling water with a drizzle of vinegar. No salt. Boil for 2½ minutes. Shock in ice water. Serve on salads.

pochés [poh-SHAY] (see poached)
Poached.

quiche [KEESH]
French origin. Roll out flaky pastry dough into tart pan. Alternatively use puff pastry. Fill tart shell with sautéed vegetables, meat, or other fillings. Make a custard using 1 egg per cup of cream, half and half, or milk. Salt and pepper to taste. Add nutmeg. Pour custard over fillings. Bake at 375°F until custard is set and bottom of tart is dry.

quiche Lorraine [KEESH loh-REN]
French origin. Proceed as with quiche. Fill with sautéed diced bacon before adding custard.

Sardou [sahr-DOO]
American origin (New Orleans). Poached eggs, topped with artichoke hearts, ham, anchovies, truffles, and hollandaise.

Scotch
Mix ground pork, egg, chopped parsley, sage, thyme, ground coriander, nutmeg, salt, and pepper to taste. Make patties. Shape around hard-boiled eggs. Dip each egg in flour, then egg batter, then bread crumbs. Deep-fry or bake.

scrambled
Beat eggs. Season with salt and pepper. Cook in buttered saucepan over low heat. Constantly stir until eggs are semicoagulated yet still creamy. Serve immediately.

shirred (see baked)

soft-boiled
Plunge eggs in boiling water with a drizzle of vinegar. No salt. Boil 3 minutes. Serve immediately.

soufflé [soo-FLAY]

Start with a thick béchamel or pastry cream. Season with savory or sweet garnish and salt and pepper. Add 2 egg yolks per cup of sauce or cream. Fold in 1 whipped egg white for each egg yolk. Pour into ramekins coated with butter, sugar, or bread crumbs. Bake at 375°F until risen and golden brown on top.

souffléed omelet

Beat egg yolks and sugar. Whisk egg whites. Fold whites into the egg yolk and sugar mixture. Sauté until browned on the outside and soft and creamy inside. Fold or leave flat. (If desired, add fruit or preserve filling.)

strata

Sauté sausage, bacon, or other meat-fat garnish. Add mushrooms, onions, or other preferred garnish. Make a custard using 2 eggs per cup of milk. In a buttered oven dish, layer bread slices, garnishes, and grated cheddar cheese. Pour custard over. Bake at 350°F.

sunny-side up (see pan-fried)

sur le Plat [SER luh plah]

French origin. Break the eggs in an ovenproof, buttered ramekin. Bake in a bain-marie at 350°F until the egg white is set.

timbale [TIM-bahl]

French origin. Blanch, boil, or sauté thinly diced vegetables. Place loosely into buttered ramekin. Make a custard using 3 eggs per cup of cream. Salt and pepper to taste. Pour custard over vegetables. Bake in a bain-marie at 325°F until set. Serve warm.

tortilla de patatas [tohr-TEE-yuh day pah-TAH-tahs]

Spanish origin. Blanch and sauté potatoes in abundant olive oil. (If desired, add onions.) Mix in beaten eggs, cover, and cook very slowly to coagulate the eggs. Tortilla must be thick, not too brown, and evenly cooked. Serve warm or cold.

Western omelet

American origin. Sauté onions, green peppers, and diced ham. Add beaten eggs and make a flat omelet.

The
Chef's
Répertoire

Fish
&
Seafood

à la king
Sauté onions and garlic. Sauté mushrooms and green pepper or pimiento. Add shrimp and scallops. Add béchamel and lemon juice. (If desired, add lobster meat, peas, and scallions.) Bake au gratin.

al mojo de ajo [al moh-hoh day ah-hoh]
Mexican origin. Sauté fish filet a la plancha. Add chopped parsley and garlic. Sauté. Deglaze with lime. Serve immediately.

au bleu [oh BLEUH]
French origin. Toss freshly caught trout or salmon in vinegar. Poach in vinegary court bouillon. Garnish and serve.

beurre noir [burr NWAR]
Black butter. French origin. Sauté fish filet in clarified butter. Reserve. Add fresh butter. Let foam and cook until light brown. Add lemon juice, salt, pepper, and chopped parsley. Serve immediately.

black butter (see beurre noir)

blue trout (see au bleu)

bonne femme; à la bonne femme [bun FEHM]
French origin. Sauté or poach filet of fish such as sole. Serve with beurre blanc or velouté with sliced white mushrooms and pearl onions.

bouillabaisse [BOO-yuh-BEZ]
1. French origin (Provence). Marinate Mediterranean fish and seafood medley with olive oil, garlic, fennel, pastis, saffron, potato slices, herbes de Provence, salt, and pepper. Add seafood broth and boil for 20 minutes under high heat. Serve at once with rouille sauce and garlic crostini.
2. American version. Make a seafood broth with saffron. Add parboiled potatoes. Poach lobster and filets of fish such as sea bass, grouper, and snapper.

bourride [boo-REED]
French origin. Make a broth with white wine, tomatoes, onions, saffron, thyme, fennel, leeks and potatoes. Salt and pepper to taste. Poach monkfish. Reserve. Reduce broth. Thicken with aioli. Serve with aioli and a toasted baguette on the side.

brandade [brahn-DAHD]
French origin (Provence). Desalt salted cod. Poach. Sauté onions. Process cod, onions, and garlic. Add olive oil, cream, lemon juice, salt, and pepper. Add mashed potatoes and mix. Serve hot or cold.

cioppino [chuh-PEE-noh]
Italian-American origin. Similar to bouillabaisse. Prepare a base sauce by sautéing garlic, onions, celery, bell pepper, and Mediterranean herbs. Add vinegar, tabasco-style sauce, Worcestershire, and tomato sauce. Simmer. Poach fish such as halibut or snapper and shellfish such as scallops, shrimp, crab, clams, or mussels in base sauce.

clambake; clam bake
Native American origin. Boil clams, mussels, chicken thighs, and lobster with potatoes, corn, and onions. (If desired, add seaweed.) Finish with butter. Usually cooked in a pit in the sand.

clams oreganata
Italian origin. Open raw clams and stuff the half shell with a mixture of bread crumbs, oregano, parsley, mint, salt, pepper, and olive oil. Bake at 375°F.

crab cake
Many variations. Sauté finely chopped bell peppers, scallions, and garlic. Add mayonnaise, Dijon mustard, salt, pepper, fresh herbs, eggs, and bread crumbs. Add crab meat. Shape into patties. Sauté or bake.

crab imperial
American origin. Combine crab meat with mayonnaise or a white sauce. Spoon into blue-crab or scallop shells. Sprinkle with Parmesan and bake until golden.

crab Louis; crab Louie [LOO-ee]
American origin. Place lump crab meat on a bed of shredded lettuce. Top with a dressing of mayonnaise, cream, chili sauce, scallions, green pepper, lemon juice, herbs, and spices. Garnish with tomato and hard-boiled egg. Serve cold.

crab rangoon
American origin. Process scallions. Add crab meat and cream cheese. (If desired, add ginger, garlic, soy sauce, and Worcestershire.) Fold into won ton wrappers. Deep-fry.

Fish
&
Seafood

Dieppoise; à la Dieppoise [dee-uh-PWAHZ]
French origin. Sauté or poach filet. Garnish with shrimp, steamed mussels, and white mushrooms. Reduce poaching liquid. Add cream, salt, and pepper. Monter au beurre.

doria; à la doria
French origin. Sauté or poach filet. Garnish with sautéed tournéed cucumbers.

Dubarry; à la Dubarry [doo-BAIR-ee]
French origin. Sauté or poach filet. Sauce with Mornay. Garnish with steamed or sautéed cauliflower and pommes château.

dugléré [dew-glair-RAY]
French origin. Bake flatfish with shallots and white wine. Make a roux. Add cooking juices from the baked fish to make a velouté. Add cream, tomato concassée, and chopped parsley.

encebollado; encebollado de pescado [en-seh-boh-YAH-doh day pes-KAH-doh]
Ecuadorian origin. Make a refrito with onions, tomatoes, cumin, chili powder, garlic, and salt. Add water. Poach tuna. Add boiled yucca. Serve with lime and avocado garnish.

en papillote [ahn pah-pee-YOHT]
French origin. Place filet of fish such as salmon, cod, sea bass, or sole on lightly oiled parchment paper. Season with salt and pepper, spices, and fresh herbs. Add white wine, butter or olive oil, and vegetables such as shallots, asparagus, peas, or carrots julienne. Carefully seal the parchment envelope to prevent steam from escaping. Bake in oven for 5 minutes. Serve immediately.

escabèche [es-kah-BESH]
Spanish origin. International variations. Fry fish. Marinate overnight in vinegar (or half vinegar and half white wine) with chopped onions, tomatoes, parsley, carrots, celery, garlic, fennel seeds, salt, whole peppercorns, and herbs such as oregano, rosemary, thyme, and bay leaves. (If desired, add capers.) Serve chilled as an appetizer or as tapas.

étouffée; à l'étouffée [ay-too-FAY]
Cajun origin. Start with dark, thick, spicy brown roux. Add cayenne pepper, onions, green peppers, celery, garlic, salt, and pepper. Add fish stock, crawfish, and sherry. Serve over rice.

fanesca [fah-NES-kah]
Ecuadorian origin. Desalt salted cod. Make a refrito with onions, garlic, achiote, cumin, and oregano. Add cooked rice, zucchini, and butternut squash. Process until smooth. Add cabbage, fava beans, peas, corn, lima, and cannellini beans, roasted peanuts, milk, and cod. Simmer. Add queso fresco or cream cheese. Serve with sides of hard-boiled eggs, pickled onions, fried plantains, slices of queso fresco or cream cheese, hot sauce, and cheese empanadas.

fish and chips
British origin. Skin on or off. Make batter of 2 cups flour, 1 tablespoon baking powder, salt, pepper, 1 bottle brown beer, and cornstarch. Dip haddock or cod filet in batter and fry in peanut oil. Serve with thick homemade fries. Sprinkle with salt and malt vinegar.

fish boil
Scandinavian origin. Boil salted water. Add onions and whole potatoes. (If desired, add other vegetables.) Add whitefish cut into large cross-section chunks. Skim fat and serve.

Florentine; à la Florentine [FLOHR-uhn-teen]
French origin. Sauté or poach filet. Garnish with wilted spinach.

Fra Diavolo [frah DYAH-voh-loh]
Italian-American origin. Sauté onions, peppers, and garlic. Add peeled, seeded tomatoes, tomato paste, and chili pepper. Salt to taste. Simmer. Serve with seafood or pasta.

fritto misto [FREE-toh MEES-toh]
Mixed fry. Italian origin. Beer-batter bite-size servings of shrimp, sea scallops, squid, and fish. Deep- or pan-fry. Toss with lemon juice. Serve with tartar sauce or equivalent.

kiev [kee-EV]
French origin. Make a maître d'hôtel compound butter. Roll Dover sole or flounder filets around the chilled butter. Secure with toothpick. Dredge in flour, egg, and bread crumbs. Sauté.

lobster à la Delmonico (see lobster Newberg)

lobster à la Wenberg (see lobster Newberg)

lobster américaine; à l'américaine [ah la-may-ree-KEN]
French origin. Sauté, grill, poach, or roast lobster. Serve with truffles and sauce américaine.

lobster Newberg
American origin. Half lobster lengthwise. Remove meat. Sauté with paprika, salt, and pepper. Flambé with cognac. Deglaze with Madeira. Thicken with cream and egg yolk. (If available, add tomalley and coral.) Add a touch of cayenne pepper.

lobster Paul Bert; à la Paul Bert [pawl BAIR]
Half lobster lengthwise. Remove meat. Separately boil the half shell and reserve for presentation. Sauté meat with chopped shallots, shrimp, and walnuts. (If available, add tomalley and coral.) Add a béchamel sauce thickened with egg yolks. Add lemon juice and chopped parsley. Place in half shell and serve.

lobster Thermidor [THER-mi-dohr]
French origin. Half lobster lengthwise and remove meat. Sauté meat. Make a butter, cream, sherry, and Dijon mustard sauce thickened with egg yolks. Mix sauce with lobster meat. (If available, add tomalley and coral.) Place in half shell. Top with Gruyère. Bake until brown.

maître d'hôtel [MEH-truh doh-TEL]
French origin. Cream butter. Add thinly chopped shallots, parsley, salt, pepper, cayenne pepper, and lemon juice. Shape and chill. To serve, slice cold butter and place on grilled fish or seafood.

matelote [MA-tuh-loht]
French origin. Sauté bacon, onions, and garlic. Make a soft roux. Deglaze with red wine. Add fish stock, seasonings, mushrooms, and pearl onions. Poach freshwater fish such as eel, perch, or trout.

meunière [muhn-YAIR]
French origin. Sauté filet in clarified butter. Reserve fish. Add fresh butter. Heat until light brown and foamy. Deglaze with lemon juice. Add fresh chopped parsley.

mussels marinière [mah-reen-YAIR]
French origin. Steam mussels in dutch oven with a little white wine, chopped shallots, and parsley. Once mussels open, plate them. Reduce sauce. Add butter and pour sauce over mussels. Serve immediately.

Niçoise; à la Niçoise [nee-SWAHZ]
French origin. Sauté garlic and onions. Add capers, tomato concassée, salt, pepper, anchovies, and black olives. Sear fish and add to sauce.

Normande; à la Normande [nohr-MAHND]
French origin (Normandy). Sauté or poach filet such as sole. Garnish with poached oysters, steamed mussels, white mushrooms, and crawfish tails. (If desired, add truffles and toast points.)

orly [OR lee]
French origin. Dredge filet in flour, beaten eggs, and bread crumbs. Deep-fry. Serve tomato sauce on the side.

paella de marisco [pigh-AY-yuh day mah-REES-koh]
Spanish origin. Proceed as with paella mixta. Replace meat with lobster, cuttlefish, or shrimp.

paella mixta [pigh-AY-yuh MIKS-ta]
Spanish origin. Heat a paellera. Sauté chicken thighs, chorizo, garlic, onions, and red peppers. Add short-grain rice and coat with cooking oil. Add broth (twice the volume of rice), tomatoes, saffron, shrimp, and mussels. Cook until broth evaporates.

paella Valenciana [pigh-AY-yuh vah-len-see-ah-nuh]
Spanish origin (Valencia). Heat up paellera. Sauté chicken thighs, rabbit, chorizo, garlic, onions, and red peppers. Add short-grain rice and coat with cooking oil. Add broth (twice the volume of rice), green beans, fava beans, tomatoes, saffron, shrimp, and mussels. Cook until broth evaporates.

Provençal [proh-vahn-SAHL] **fish soup**
French origin (Provence). Sauté mirepoix with a variety of whole fish and seafood. Add tomato paste. Deglaze with pastis or white wine. Reduce. Add water or fish stock, saffron, and salt and pepper. Simmer. Process through a food mill. Serve with garlic crostini and rouille.

Romana; alla Romana
Italian origin (Rome). Sauté garlic and pepper flakes. Add squid. Deglaze with white wine. Reduce. Add crushed tomatoes and parsley. Reduce. Add clams and fish. Simmer. Season with salt and pepper.

Fish
&
Seafood

shrimp creole
Creole origin. Sauté peppers, onions, and celery with chili powder. Add tomatoes, tabasco-style sauce, Worcestershire, salt, and pepper. Simmer. Add shrimp. Serve over rice.

shrimp deJonghe [duh-zhong]
American origin (Chicago). Toss shrimp with softened butter, chopped garlic, shallots, salt, pepper, and chopped parsley. Place in an ovenproof dish. Add wine and bread crumbs. Bake.

shrimp scampi
Italian-American origin. Sauté prawns, lobster, or jumbo shrimp with garlic. Salt and pepper to taste. Deglaze with dry vermouth. Add lemon juice and chopped parsley. Serve over pasta.

sole amandine [AH-mahn-deen]
Flour filets or whole fish. Sauté in clarified butter. Reserve. Add fresh butter and toast almonds. Heat until light brown and foamy. Deglaze with lemon juice. Pour mixture over fish. Add fresh chopped parsley.

sole Edward VII
Bake sole with butter, almonds, chopped mushrooms, lemon juice, chopped parsley, and white wine. Salt and pepper to taste.

sole normande [nohr-MAHND]
French origin (Normandy). Sauté or poach sole. Make a normande sauce with white wine velouté, mussels, mushrooms, and shallots. (If desired, add shrimp, scallops, crawfish tails, truffles, or toast points.) Reduce. Finish with cream or crème fraîche.

truite au bleu [trew-EET oh BLEUH] (see au bleu)
Blue trout.

Veracruz; à la Veracruzana
Mexican origin. Sauté garlic and onions. Add crushed tomatoes and herbs. Simmer and reduce. Add olives, capers, salt, and pepper. Bake fish with sauce.

Véronique [vay-roh-NEEK]
French origin. Poach filet in fumet. Reserve. Sauté shallots and white grapes. Deglaze with wine. Add reduced fumet. Thicken with cream. Garnish with white grapes.

Fish
&
Seafood

The Chef's Répertoire

Meats & Poultry

adobo [ah-DOH-boh]
Spanish origin. Latin American and Asian-Pacific variations. Soak dried, red Anaheim chili peppers. Process with garlic, cumin, oregano, peppercorns, coriander, cinnamon, and apple-cider vinegar into a smooth paste. Marinate meat. Braise with onions and tomatoes until fork-tender.

alsacienne; à l'alsacienne [al-zah-SYEN]
French origin (Northeast). Meat braised with sauerkraut, potatoes, and sausage.

ancienne; à l'ancienne [ahn-SYEN]
French origin. Sauté, grill, or roast meat. Serve with braised pearl onions and sautéed mushrooms. Sauce with demi-glace.

andalouse; à l'andalouse [ahn-dah-LOOZ]
French origin. Sauté, grill, or roast meat. Serve with rice stuffed bell peppers, sautéed eggplants, and tomato concassée. Sauce with demi-glace.

Argenteuil; à l'Argenteuil [ahr-zhahn-TOY-eh]
French origin. Sauté, grill, or roast meat. Serve with asparagus. Sauce with demi-glace.

arroz con pollo [ah-ROHS kohn POH-yoh]
Rice with chicken. Spanish/Latin American origin. Marinate chicken with oregano, cumin, white pepper, and vinegar. Sear chicken in annatto or olive oil. Make a sofrito with diced onions, peppers, garlic, and tomatoes. Add water, wine, tomato paste, salt, and pepper. (If desired, add saffron.) Simmer. Cook Valencia-style rice with annatto seeds and chicken fat. Add peas and pimientos.

au jus [oh ZHOO]
French origin. Roast beef, veal, or poultry. Reserve. Caramelize cooking juices. Deglaze with water or wine. Salt and pepper to taste.

baby's head (see steak and kidney pudding)

ballotine [bal-oh-TEEN]
French origin. Debone duck or chicken leg or breast. Pound to flatten. Stuff with ground chicken, herbs, vegetables brunoise, salt, and pepper. Roll in cheesecloth and secure with butcher string. Poach in stock. Serve warm or chilled.

bangers and mash
British origin. Pork sausages served with mash potatoes.

barbacoa [bahr-bah-KOH-ah]
Mexican origin. Many variations. Rub bone-in beef chuck roast with garlic, oregano, and chile powder. Salt and pepper to taste. Wrap in banana leaves. Slow cook in water smoker for 4 to 6 hours. Add soaked hardwood chips. (If desired, serve with beans and hearty vegetable soup.)

Basque chicken (see poulet basquaise)

beef à la mode
French origin. Sear large piece of beef such as sirloin. Braise with beef stock, red wine, and dried herbs. Add tournéed or large-diced celery, carrots, and onions. Braise until beef is cooked medium-rare and vegetables are tender. Rest meat. Reserve vegetables. Reduce sauce. Assemble and serve.

beef Bourguignon [boor-gee-NYON] (see boeuf bourguignon)

beef braciole (see braciola)

beef burgundy (see boeuf Bourguignon)

beef stroganov (see stroganoff)

beef tartare [tar-TAR]
French origin. Grind raw lean beef such as tenderloin. Season with salt, pepper, tabasco-style sauce, Worcestershire, and Dijon mustard. Shape into a mound. Place a raw egg yolk on the top. Garnish with chopped parsley, shallots, capers, and gherkins.

beef Wellington
French origin. Make a mushroom duxelle by sautéing finely chopped mushroom and chopped shallots in white wine. Reduce to a dry consistency. Mix duxelle with ground chicken, 2 eggs, and foie gras. Sear whole beef tenderloin. Season with salt and pepper. Rest beef 20 minutes. Brush with egg whites. Coat with duxelle mixture. Lay out a sheet of puff pastry, large enough to wrap the whole tenderloin, and brush with egg whites. Wrap the tenderloin. Decorate with egg wash and puff pastry scraps. Bake for 30 minutes in a 425°F convection oven. Rest 15 minutes before serving.

Beijing duck (see Peking duck)

Meats
&
Poultry

bibimbap [be-beem-bop]
Korean origin. Boil rice. Wilt spinach. Sauté bean sprouts. Sauté
julienned zucchini. Stir-fry kosari. Sauté shitake mushrooms. Sauté
ground beef and season with soy sauce, garlic, sugar, and peppers.
Sauté julienned carrots. Prepare egg sunny-side up. To assemble, place
rice in the middle of a large platter and display vegetables and meat
around it. Place egg on top. Drizzle with sesame oil and chili oil.
Serve immediately.

bigarade [bee-gah-RAHD]
French origin. Braise duck. Reduce braising stock with orange and
lemon juice. (If desired, thicken with roux.) Monter au beurre.
Garnish with confit of julienned orange and lemon.

blanquette [blahn-KET] (see blanquette de veau)

blanquette de veau [blahn-KET duh voh]
French origin. Poach cubed veal in broth with mirepoix. Reserve
when fork-tender. Thicken broth with white roux and egg yolks.
Finish with lemon juice, salt, and pepper. Pour over veal. Add glazed
pearl onions and sautéed mushrooms.

boeuf Bourguignon [buwf boor-gee-NYON]
French origin. Marinate beef cubes in red wine and mirepoix overnight.
Pat-dry. Sauté. Add flour to make a roux. Deglaze with marinade.
Add mirepoix, herbs, garlic, salt, and pepper. Braise until meat is fork-
tender. Garnish with sautéed bacon and sautéed mushrooms.

boeuf en daube [buwf ahn DOHB] (see daube)

boeuf ficelle [buwf fee-SEL]
French origin. Make a broth with beef broth, mirepoix, bay leaves,
and garlic. Tie whole boneless rib-eye with butcher twine. Attach
one end to the pot handle in order to raise and lower beef into the
poaching liquid. Poach beef to medium-rare. Serve with horseradish
sauce, boiled potatoes, and vegetables.

Bordelaise [bohr-duh-LEZ]
French origin. Roast, grill, or sauté meat. Make Bordelaise sauce by
reducing chopped shallots, coarse peppercorns, thyme, bay leaf, and
red Bordeaux. Add demi-glace. (If desired, pass through chinois.) Salt
and pepper to taste.

Meats
&
Poultry

bowl o'red (see Texas chili)

braciola [bra-chee-OH-lah]
Italian origin. Similar to involtini. Pound beef round steaks. Dredge in bread crumbs, grated Pecorino-Romano, chopped parsley, and garlic. Salt and pepper to taste. Roll up and skewer or tie with butcher twine. Sauté, grill, or roast.

Brunswick stew
American origin. Sauté onions and bacon. Sear beef and chicken. Add cooked ham and water. Salt and pepper to taste. Simmer. Add tomatoes, potatoes, and corn. Simmer. Finish with okra, lima beans, and green beans. Serve immediately.

bubble and squeak
British origin. Sauté onions and cabbage until soft and translucent. Fold in mashed potatoes. Shape into individual cakes. Sauté until browned.

Buffalo wings
American origin (Buffalo, New York). Many variations. Toss wings in flour. Deep fry at 375°F. When fully cooked, toss wings in melted butter, red-wine vinegar, and hot red-pepper sauce. Serve with celery sticks and blue cheese dressing.

cacciatora [ka-chuh-TOHR-uh] (see cacciatore)

cacciatore; alla cacciatore [ka-chuh-TOHR-eh]
Italian origin. Sauté chicken. Sauté mushrooms and chopped shallots. Deglaze with Chianti. Add demi-glace, tomatoes, and chopped parsley.

canard à l'orange [KA-narhd ah loh-ranzh]
Duck with orange sauce. French origin. Braise whole duck and reduce braising stock with orange and lemon juice. Make a gastrique (caramel and vinegar) sauce with the duck braising stock. Garnish with confit of julienned orange and lemon and orange supreme.

carbonade [KAHR-boh-nahd]
1. French origin. Regional variations. Sauté beef chunks in a Dutch oven. Reserve. Sauté onions. Return beef to pan. Make a roux. Deglaze with dark beer. Add beef stock. Simmer until meat is fork-tender. Salt and pepper to taste.
(continued...)

Meats
&
Poultry

2. Belgian origin. Sauté dry beef cubes. Add flour to make a roux. Deglaze with beer. Add sautéed mirepoix, herbs, garlic, salt, and pepper. Braise until meat is fork-tender. Add sautéed onions. Garnish with sautéed bacon and sautéed mushrooms.

carbonade à la flamande [KAHR-boh-nahd ah lah FLAH-mahnde] (see carbonade)

cassoulet [ka-soo-LAY]
French origin (Southwest). Soak haricot blancs, lingots, or navy beans overnight. Sauté mirepoix in duck fat. Add soaked beans. Simmer. Add duck confit, garlic, cubed cured pork meat, sausages, herbs, salt, and pepper. When done, broil in oven.

cazuela [ka-zway-lah]
Spanish/South American origin. Many regional variations. Traditionally cooked in earthenware. Braise beef, chicken, or pork with potatoes and pumpkin. (If desired, add cooked rice, noodles, green beans, celery, carrots, or corn.)

charcutière [CHAHR-koo-TYAIR]
French origin. Sauté pork chops. Sauce with charcutière sauce. (If desired, add mashed potatoes.)

chasseur [shah-SUR]
French origin. Sauté chicken. Reserve. Sauté mushrooms and chopped shallots. Deglaze with white wine. Reduce. Add demi-glace and tomatoes. Add chicken and simmer until fork-tender. Salt and pepper to taste. (If desired add chopped parsley.)

chicken à la king
Poach chicken pieces in broth. Simmer. Make a roux by starting a velouté and adding cream. Add sautéed mushrooms. Thicken with egg yolks. Serve in puff pastry shells.

chicken Chardonnay [shar-doh-NAY]
Dredge chicken in flour. Sauté and reserve. Sauté onions and leeks. Deglaze with Chardonnay. Add stock and reduce. Add cream. Salt and pepper to taste. Monter au beurre.

chicken coq au vin [kok oh VEHN] (see coq au vin)

chicken cordon bleu [kor-dohn BLEUH]
Pound chicken breast. Salt and pepper. Top with ham and Gruyère.
Fold. Dredge in flour, then eggs, and then bread crumbs. Sauté.

chicken fricassee [FRIHK-uh-see]
American origin (Louisiana). Marinate chicken pieces in Cajun spices
and herbs. Sauté. Make a brown roux. Add onions, celery, red and
green peppers, and andouille sausage. Add chicken stock, tomato
paste, and Worcestershire. Serve with rice.

chicken Kiev [kee-EV]
Cream butter with salt, pepper, lemon juice, chopped parsley, chives,
and garlic. Shape in parchment paper and chill. Pound chicken breast.
Salt and pepper. Enclose butter while folding chicken breasts. Dredge
packets in flour, then eggs, and then bread crumbs. Sauté.

chicken paprikash [PAH-pree-kash]
Hungarian origin. Sauté chicken pieces. Sauté onions. Make a roux.
Add paprika and chicken stock. Salt and pepper to taste. Simmer.
Finish with sour cream and lemon juice. Serve with spaetzle.

chicken pot pie
Poach chicken pieces in broth. Simmer. Make a roux by starting a
velouté and adding cream. Add mirepoix and peas. Finish with salt
and pepper, lemon juice, and nutmeg.

chicken Tetrazzini [te-trah-ZEE-nee] (see Tetrazzini)

chicken tikka [TEE-kah]
Indian origin. Dry-rub chicken pieces with red chili pepper, cumin,
coriander, ginger, turmeric, and garam masala. Marinate in yogurt,
lime, and white vinegar. Pat-dry. Skewer. Grill or roast in tandoor oven.

chicken tikka masala [TEE-kah muh-SAH-lah]
Indian-British origin. Many variations. Dry-rub chicken pieces with
red chili pepper, cumin, coriander, ginger, turmeric, and garam
masala. Marinate overnight in yogurt, lime, and white vinegar. Pat-
dry. Skewer. Grill or roast in tandoor oven. Make a sauce with sautéed
onions, cardamom, garam masala, brown sugar, tomatoes, and
almonds. Reduce. Finish with cream.

Meats
&
Poultry

chili con carne [chee-lee kohn KAHR-nay]
Sauté small diced beef chuck and season with chili powder. Sauté onions, chili peppers, and garlic. Add crushed tomatoes. Simmer until meat is fork-tender. Serve with pasta, beans, or rice. (If desired, add sour cream.)

chop suey [chop SOO-ee]
American origin (San Francisco). Stir-fry chicken, beef, pork, fish, or shrimp. Reserve. Stir-fry vegetables such as water chestnuts, mushrooms, bean sprouts, onions, peppers, or bamboo shoots until crisp-tender. Reserve. Make a sauce by mixing hot chili paste, soy sauce, oyster sauce, and scallions. (If desired, thicken with starch.) Add meat and vegetables to sauce. Serve over rice.

chow fun [chow foon]
Chinese origin. American variations. Stir-fry meat such as chicken, pork, beef, or duck. Reserve. Stir-fry vegetables such as carrots, peppers, mushrooms. Add Chinese ho fun (wide rice) noodles, soy sauce, and oyster sauce thickened with cornstarch. Serve immediately.

chow mein [chow MAYN]
Chinese origin. American variations. Stir-fry chicken, pork, beef, or duck meat. Reserve. Stir-fry Asian-cut carrots, peppers, water chestnuts, bamboo shoots, and mushrooms. Add fried Chinese egg noodles, soy sauce, and oyster sauce thickened with cornstarch. Serve immediately.

civet [Eng. SIV-it] [Fr. see-VAY]
French origin. Sauté rabbit, venison, wild boar, or jackrabbit pieces with mirepoix. Add flour to make a roux. Add brown stock. Add garlic and bouquet garni. Simmer. Garnish with glazed pearl onions, sautéed bacon, and mushrooms. Thicken with pork blood. Do not boil.

Clamart; à la Clamart [kla-MAHR]
French origin. Sauté, grill, or roast a piece of meat. Serve with green peas and artichokes.

cocotte [koh-KOT]
French origin. Served with glazed pearl onions, sautéed mushrooms, and tournéed vegetables cocotte sauced with demi-glace.

confit [kon-FEE]
French origin (Southwest). Salt duck legs, goose legs, or ham for 24 hours to cure. Rinse well. Pat-dry. Slow-poach meat in duck or goose fat seasoned with garlic, bay leaves, and black peppercorns at 170°F to 200°F until fork-tender. Reserve meat in the fat for later use. To serve, broil legs or ham until crispy. Variation: Serve cold with a salad.

coq au vin [kok-oh-VEHN]
French origin. Marinate chicken pieces in red wine. Sauté chicken. Sauté mirepoix. Make a roux. Deglaze with marinade and reduce. Add chicken stock, tomato paste, herbs, salt, and pepper. Simmer. Add sautéed mushrooms and glazed pearl onions. (If desired, add sautéed bacon.)

corned beef hash
Sauté diced onions. Add diced, leftover corned beef. Add leftover vegetables such as potatoes, carrots, parsnips, and turnips. Compress in hot pan to make a crust. Flip and make a crust on the other side. Usually served with eggs.

cottage pie
British origin. Sauté mirepoix. Add ground beef. Add tomato paste and simmer. Salt and pepper to taste. (If desired, add peas.) Place in ovenproof dish. Pipe mashed potatoes on top. Bake at 375°F.

country captain
American origin (Southern). Sear chicken with curry, ginger, and chili peppers. Reserve. Sauté onions, bell peppers, and garlic. Add chicken stock, tomatoes, and apples. Add chicken and simmer.

crapaudine [kra-poh-DEEN]
French origin. Fabricate chicken by removing dorsal spine. Open like a book and remove bones from the thoracic chamber. Salt and pepper to taste. Toss in herbs, spices, and oil. Grill.

creamed chicken
Poach chicken pieces in broth. Simmer. Make a roux by starting a velouté and adding cream. Finish with salt, pepper, lemon juice, and nutmeg.

Crécy; à la Crécy [KRAY-see]
French origin. Sauté, grill, or roast a piece of meat. Serve with carrots.

curry
Indian origin. Many variations. Pan-fry curry spices such as turmeric, red chili powder, coriander, cumin, fenugreek, pepper, allspice, nutmeg, mace, and cardamom in ghee or oil. Sear meat. Sauté grated onions. Deglaze with water. Add tomatoes. Simmer until meat is tender.

dal; dhal; dhall [DAHL]
Indian origin. Soak and boil chick peas, mung beans, lentils, black-eyed peas, and other beans. Pan-fry garam masala with onions. Add chopped tomatoes and yogurt. Add cooked beans. Sprinkle with cilantro and serve.

daube [DOHB]
French origin. Marinate cubed beef in red or white wine and mirepoix overnight. Pat-dry. Sauté. Transfer to clay pot. Add carrots, mirepoix, marinade, orange peel, herbs, and garlic. Cover and slow-bake until meat is fork-tender.

diable; à la diable [dee-AH-bluh]
French origin. Sauté, grill, or roast meat. Sauce with diable sauce.

Dijonnaise; à la Dijonnaise [dee-zhah-NEZ]
French origin. Roast, grill, or sauté meat. Add sauce of choice. Finish sauce with Dijon mustard.

dirty steak
Sear steak directly on hot coals. Salt and pepper to taste.

doner-kebab; doner-kabob [DUH-ner kuh-BOB]
Middle Eastern origin. Skewer thin slices of lamb, beef, chicken or pork, superposed with ground lamb, beef, chicken, or pork on a vertical rotisserie. Cook meat. Serve on pita bread. (If desired, add tomatoes, onions, lettuce, and yogurt-based sauce.)

doria; à la doria
French origin. Sauté meat. Garnish with sautéed tournéed cucumbers.

Dubarry; à la Dubarry [doo-BAIR-ee]
French origin. Sauté meat. Sauce with Mornay. Garnish with steamed or sautéed cauliflower and pommes château.

enchilada [en-chee-LAH-dah]
Mexican origin. Wrap soft corn tortilla around meat, cheese, beans, potatoes, vegetables, fish, or any combination of filling. Top with chili pepper sauce.

espagnole; à l'espagnole [es-pah-NYOHL]
French origin. Diced tomatoes, onions, garlic, and sweet peppers. Served as an accompaniment for Spanish-style meat dishes.

estouffade [ES-too-fahd]
French origin. Marinate cubed beef in red wine and mirepoix overnight. Pat-dry. Sauté. Add flour to make a roux. Deglaze with marinade. Add mirepoix, herbs, garlic, tomatoes, salt, and pepper. Braise until meat is fork-tender. Garnish with sautéed bacon and olives.

etouffade [AY-too-fahd] (see estouffade)

fajitas [fa-HEE-tuhs]
Mexican origin. Marinate skirt steak with oil, lime juice, red pepper, and garlic. Grill. Slice into strips. Wrap in warm, soft corn tortilla. Serve with grilled onions and peppers, guacamole, refried beans, salsa, or a combination of these items.

farsumagru [fahr-soo-MAH-groo]
Italian origin (Sicily). Pound veal into rectangular shape. Top with slices of prosciutto and mortadella, hard-boiled eggs, diced cheese, minced garlic, ground meat, peas, and Italian sausage. Roll up and tie with butcher string. Roast. Rest. Serve with demi-glace.

financière; à la financière [feen-ahn-SYAIR]
French origin. Sauté meat. Garnish with truffles, mushrooms, and olives mixed with Madeira sauce.

fiorentina; alla fiorentina [fyohr-en-TEEN-uh]
Italian origin. Grill porterhouse steak to rare or medium-rare. Salt and pepper to taste.

flamande, à la flamande [flah-MAHND]
French origin. Meat accompaniment made of braised cabbage, carrots, turnips, potatoes, and sometimes pork or sausages.

Florentine; à la Florentine [FLOHR-uhn-teen]
French origin. Sauté meat. Garnish with wilted spinach. (If desired, add Mornay sauce.)

fondue, Burgundy
French origin. Tableside, fry cubed beef tenderloin in hot oil. Serve with variety of sauces such as Béarnaise, aïoli, or choron.

Meats
&
Poultry

fondue, cheese

Swiss origin. Bring 1½ cups white wine to a boil with a clove of garlic, then simmer. Add 1 tablespoon cornstarch and 2 teaspoons kirsch. Gradually add 1 lb grated cheese such as Swiss or Emmental. Do not boil. Served with bite-sized French bread.

fondue, chocolate

Bring 1 cup heavy cream to a boil. Remove from heat and add 14 oz of chocolate. Process for smoothness. Add liquor. Serve warm with diced fruits such as bananas, strawberries, or pineapple.

forestière; à la forestière [foh-res-TYAIR]

French origin. Accompaniment or sauce made of diced potatoes, bacon, and wild mushrooms.

francese [frahn-CHAY-suh]

Italian origin. Dredge scaloppine in flour, then eggs. Salt and pepper to taste. Sauté. Finish with a drizzle of lemon juice and fresh parsley.

fricassée [free-kah-SAY]

French origin. Sauté chicken pieces and mirepoix without browning. Make a white roux. Deglaze with white wine. Add chicken stock. Simmer until meat is fork-tender. Finish sauce with cream. Salt and pepper to taste.

fried chicken

American origin (Southern). Marinate chicken pieces in buttermilk, salt, and pepper. Dredge chicken in flour and red pepper. Pan-fry.

galantine [gah-lahn-TEEN]

French origin. Debone duck or chicken. Marinate in brandy. Stuff with ground veal or pork, bacon, herbs, pistachios, salt, and pepper. (If desired, add truffles.) Roll in a cheese cloth and secure with butcher string. Poach in stock. Serve chilled.

garbure [gar-BYUR]

French origin (Southwest). Precook cabbage in duck fat. Start soup with salt pork, precooked cabbage, onions, carrots, turnips, white beans, and herbs. Salt and pepper to taste. Simmer for 2 hours. To finish, add confit d'oie (goose legs in rendered fat).

Meats
&
Poultry

gardiane [gahr-DYAN]
French origin. Similar to daube, but made with bull meat. Marinate beef cubes in red or white wine and mirepoix overnight. Pat-dry. Sauté. Transfer to clay pot. Add carrots, mirepoix, marinade, orange peel, herbs, and garlic. Cover and slow-bake until meat is fork-tender.

goulash [GOO-lahsh]
Hungarian origin. Sauté onions. Sauté beef with paprika. Add stock and simmer. Add halved potatoes, tomatoes, and green peppers. Simmer. Serve with dumplings and sour cream.

grand-mère [GRAHN mair]
French origin. Sauté chicken quarters. Sauté bacon, pearl onions, and mushrooms. Deglaze with white wine. Add stock. Salt and pepper to taste. Simmer 45 minutes.

grand veneur [GRAHN vuh-nur]
French origin. Marinate venison overnight. Braise. Serve with chestnut purée and grand veneur sauce.

gumbo [GUHM-boh]
Sear deboned chicken with ground red pepper. Reserve. Make a brown roux. Add celery, onions, green bell peppers, and chicken stock. Bring to a boil. Add seared chicken and andouille sausage. Simmer until cooked through.

gumbo ya ya [GUHM-boh YAH-YAH]
American origin (Louisiana). Similar to gumbo. Sear deboned chicken and reserve. Make a brown roux. Add onions, celery, green bell peppers, and cayenne pepper. Salt and pepper to taste. Add stock and simmer. Add garlic, andouille sausage, and seared chicken. Simmer until chicken is tender.

gyro [YEE-roh]
Greek origin. Shaved slices of spiced roasted lamb, beef, or chicken on a pita with yogurt-based sauce. Marinated beef or chicken may be used. (If desired use grilled onions, sweet peppers, and tomatoes.)

involtini [een-VOHL-tee-nee]
Italian origin. Pound veal cutlets. Dredge in bread crumbs, grated Pecorino-Romano, chopped parsley, and garlic. Salt and pepper to taste. Roll up and skewer or tie with butcher twine. Sauté, grill, or roast.

Meats
&
Poultry

Irish stew
  Irish origin. Sauté onions. Add lamb shoulder pieces without
  browning. Add halved potatoes, chicken stock, and Worcestershire.
  Salt and pepper to taste. Simmer. Add carrots and pearl barley.
  Simmer until meat is tender.

Jamaican jerk chicken
  Jamaican origin. Make a marinade with lime juice, habañero, white
  vinegar, fresh herbs, and spices. Marinate chicken. Pat-dry. Grill.

jambalaya [juhm-buh-LIGH-yah], **Cajun**
  American origin (Louisiana). Regional variations. Sauté andouille and
  chicken or pork until well-browned. Reserve. Sauté vegetables such
  as celery and red and green peppers with Cajun spices. (Do not use
  tomatoes.) Add shrimp or other seafood, sautéed andouille, and meat
  of choice, 1 volume of medium-grain rice, and 2 volumes of chicken
  stock. Simmer until rice is cooked.

jambalaya [juhm-buh-LIGH-yah], **Creole**
  American origin (Louisiana). Regional variations. Sauté andouille
  and chicken or pork. Reserve. Sauté vegetables such as celery, red and
  green peppers, and tomatoes with Creole spices. Add shrimp or other
  seafood, sautéed andouille, chicken, 1 volume of medium-grain rice,
  and 2 volumes of chicken stock mixed with or without tomato sauce.
  Simmer until rice is cooked.

jambalaya [juhm-buh-LIGH-yah], **red** (see jambalaya, Creole)

kari; kare; karee [KAH-ree] (see curry)

Kate and Sidney pie (see steak and kidney pie)

kibbeh [KIH-beh]**; kibbi; kibbe** [KIH-bee]
  Middle Eastern origin (Syria). Many regional variations. Mix bulgur,
  chopped onions, and ground lamb. (If desired, add spices and herbs
  such as mint.) Shape into meatballs or torpedoes. Deep-fry. Variation:
  Shape in a sheet pan and bake.

korma [KHOR-mah]
  Indian origin. British variations. Pan-fry herbs such as cardamom
  seeds, cinnamon, red chili pepper, cumin, and cloves. Sauté onions.
  Sauté chicken. Add tomato sauce and buttermilk. Simmer.

lapin à la moutarde [LA-pehn ah lah MOO-tahrd]
French origin. Marinate rabbit pieces with Dijon mustard overnight.
Sear rabbit and reserve. Sauté mirepoix. Return rabbit to pan. Deglaze
with white wine. Add stock and thyme. Reduce. Add cream and
simmer. Add Dijon mustard. Salt and pepper to taste.

liver and onions
Slow sauté onions without browning. Reserve. Dredge calf liver in
flour. Sauté. Deglaze with white wine and reduce. Add stock and
reduce. Finish with a drizzle of vinegar. Serve with sautéed onions.

lo mein [loh MAYN]
Chinese origin. Many variations. Stir-fry chicken, pork, beef, or duck
meat. Reserve. Stir-fry Asian-cut carrots, peppers, and mushrooms.
Add Chinese egg noodles, soy sauce, and oyster sauce thickened with
cornstarch. Serve immediately.

Madras
Indian origin. Sauté chicken, lamb, or beef. Reserve. Sauté onions
with ginger, garlic, garam masala, and chile powder. Add chopped,
peeled and seeded tomatoes. Hand-blend. Add coconut milk. Simmer
until tender. Serve with rice pilaf.

maître d'hôtel [MEH-truh doh-TEL]
French origin. Cream butter. Add thinly chopped shallots, parsley,
salt, pepper, cayenne pepper, and lemon juice. Shape and chill. To
serve, slice cold butter and place on grilled meat.

Marengo [mah-REN-goh]
French origin. Sauté cubed veal until browned. Reserve. Sauté onions.
Deglaze with white wine. Add tomato concassée, stock, bouquet
garni, and veal. Simmer until fork-tender. Garnish with glazed pearl
onions, mushrooms, chopped parsley, and croutons.

meatloaf
Mix ground beef and pork, onions, bread crumbs, ketchup or tomato
sauce, chopped herbs, and eggs. Salt and pepper to taste. Force into a
mold. Bake at 350°F. Serve with mashed potatoes.

Milanaise; à la Milanaise [mee-lah-NEZ]
French/Italian origin. Dredge scallopine in flour, then eggs, and then
Parmigiano-Reggiano and bread crumbs. Salt and pepper to taste.
Sauté. Finish with a drizzle of lemon juice and fresh parsley.

Meats
&
Poultry

milanesas [mee-lah-NAY-suhs]
South American/Italian origin. Similar to Wiener Schnitzel. Dredge scallopine in flour, then eggs, and then bread crumbs. Salt and pepper to taste. Sauté. Finish with a drizzle of lemon juice and fresh parsley.

moussaka; mousaka [moo-SAH-kah]
Greek origin. Many regional variations, notably in the Middle East, the Balkans, and Turkey. Sauté eggplant slices in olive oil. Layer with cooked ground lamb, onions, and tomatoes. Top with béchamel sauce. (If desired, add cheese.) Bake.

Nantua; à la Nantua [nan-TWAH]
French origin. Poach filets. Garnish with crawfish tails. (If desired, add truffles.) Serve with Nantua sauce.

navarin [na-vah-rehn]
French origin. Sauté cubed lamb until well-browned. Sauté mirepoix or other vegetables. Add flour and make a brown roux. Deglaze with brandy, water, or brown stock. Add brown stock and herbs. Salt and pepper to taste. Add turned turnips. Simmer until meat is fork-tender.

navarin printanier [na-vah-rehn prehn-tahn-YAY]
French origin. Sauté cubed lamb until well-browned. Sauté mirepoix or other vegetables. Add flour and make a brown roux. Deglaze with brandy, water or brown stock. Add brown stock and herbs. Salt and pepper to taste. Add spring vegetables such as baby turnips, baby carrots, pearl onions, and pommes cocotte. Simmer until meat is fork-tender.

negimaki [NAH-gee-MAH-kee]
Japanese origin. Pound out thin slices of steak. Roll steak around flash-blanched scallions. Secure with toothpicks. Instant-marinate in teriyaki sauce and grill. Slice and serve.

New England boiled dinner
Poach corned beef. Add pearl onions, carrots, potatoes, parsnips, turnips, and green cabbage. Simmer until tender.

Niçoise; à la Niçoise [nee-SWAHZ]
French origin (Nice). Roast, grill, or sauté meat. Garnish with confit tomatoes, French green beans sautéed in butter, and pommes château.

nivernaise; à la nivernaise [nee-vair-NEZ]
French origin. Roast, grill, or sauté meat. Garnish with glazed, turned carrots and turnips, glazed pearl onions, and pommes vapeur. (If desired, add braised lettuce.)

Orloff
French origin. Braise veal loin. Slice. Top with soubise (slow-sautéed onions) and duxelle (puréed mushrooms). Sauce with Mornay. Bake au gratin. Usuaully served with side of celery purée, confite tomatoes, stuffed lettuce leaves, and pommes château.

osso bucco; osso buco [OH-soh BOO-koh] (see osso bucco Milanese)

osso bucco Milanese [OH-soh BOO-koh mee-lah-NAY-seh]
Italian origin. Sear veal shanks and reserve. Sauté mirepoix. Deglaze with white wine. Add tomato sauce, stock, and herbs. Add veal shanks and braise. Simmer until meat is fork-tender. Salt and pepper to taste.

osso bucco alla Milanese [OH-soh BOO-koh ah lah mee-lah-NAY-seh] (see osso bucco Milanese)

osso bucco in bianco [OH-soh BOO-koh een bee-AHN-koh]
Italian origin. Sear veal shanks and reserve. Sauté mirepoix with garlic and anchovies. Deglaze with white wine. Return veal shanks and braise until fork-tender. To serve, sprinkle with gremolata (chopped lemon zest, garlic, and parsley).

pad Thai [pad tigh]
Thai origin. Many variations. Stir-fry eggs, vegetables such as bean sprouts, and shrimp, chicken, or tofu. Add rice noodles. Season with soy sauce, fish sauce, chili peppers, lime, and tamarind. Add peanuts and fresh cilantro. Serve immediately.

paella mixta [pigh-AY-yuh MIKS-ta]
Spanish origin. Heat a paellera. Sauté chicken thighs, chorizo, garlic, onions, and red peppers. Add short-grain rice and coat with cooking oil. Add broth (twice the volume of rice), tomatoes, saffron, shrimp, and mussels. Cook until broth evaporates.

Meats
&
Poultry

paella Valenciana [pigh-AY-yuh vah-len-see-AH-nuh]
Spanish origin (Valencia). Heat a paellera. Sauté chicken thighs, rabbit, chorizo, garlic, onions, and red peppers. Add short-grain rice and coat with cooking oil. Add broth (twice the volume of rice), green beans, fava beans, tomatoes, saffron, shrimp, and mussels. Cook until broth evaporates.

parmigiana; alla parmigiana [pahr-mee-ZHAH-nah]
Italian origin. Dredge veal or eggplant slices in flour, then eggs, and then grated Parmigiano-Reggiano. Pan-fry. Usually served with tomato sauce.

pastitsio [pah-STEET-see-oh]
Greek origin. In ovenproof dish, layer tubular pasta with Bolongese or other meat-based sauce. Top with a nutmeg-flavored béchamel, Mornay, or egg-based custard. Sprinkle with cinnamon and cheese. Bake au gratin.

paupiette [poh-PYET]
French origin. Pound veal cutlets. Stuff with a filling such as olives and herbs, cheese, or vegetables. Salt and pepper to taste. Roll up and skewer or tie with butcher twine. Sauté, grill, or roast.

Peking duck
Blanch whole duck in boiling water. Hang to dry for 6 hours. While hanging, brush with a mix of honey, dry sherry, white vinegar, cornstarch, and hoisin sauce. Transfer to oven and bake at 350°F until duck reaches 165°F.

Périgourdine; à la Périgourdine [pair-ee-gour-DEEN]
French origin. Roast, grill, or sauté meat. Serve with Périgourdine sauce.

picadillo [pee-ka-DEE-yoh]
Latin American origin. Sauté onions, ground beef, and chorizo. Add tomatoes, herbs such as oregano, and spices such as cumin or coriander. Simmer. (If desired, add olives and potatoes.) Serve with tortillas or use as empanada filling.

Meats & Poultry

pizza, Chicago style
American origin (Chicago). Some variations. Dissolve 1 package dry
yeast into 1¼ cups warm water. Combine 2¾ cups flour,
½ cup cornmeal, 3 tablespoons olive oil, salt, and yeast mixture.
Knead. Separate into workable balls. Allow to rise 2 hours at room
temperature. Roll balls into 13-inch diameter circles. Transfer to
deep-dish pizza pans. Top with tomato sauce, cheese, pizza toppings,
and herbs. Bake on pizza stone in a 500°F oven for 20 minutes.

pizza, deep dish (see pizza, Chicago style)

pizza, Neapolitan style
Italian origin. Regional variations. Dissolve 1 teaspoon dry yeast into
3 cups warm water. Combine 9 cups of flour, salt, and yeast. Knead.
Separate into workable balls. Let rise overnight in refrigerator. Let
rise 2 hours at room temperature. Shape balls into 12-inch diameter
circles. Keep thin. Top with tomato sauce, pizza toppings, cheese, and
herbs. Bake on pizza stone in a 500°F oven for 20 minutes.

pizza, New York style (see pizza, Neapolitan style)

poivrade [pwahv-RAHD]
French origin. Marinate venison overnight. Braise. Serve with
poivrade sauce.

pot au feu [poht oh feuh]
French origin. Poach beef (shanks, rump roast, or bottom round) in
broth and onion piqué with clove. Poach turned potatoes, turned
carrots, turned turnips, and leeks in broth. Reserve. Serve with side of
coarse sea salt, Dijon mustard, and gherkins.

potée [POH-tay]
French origin. Regional variations. Poach ham in broth and onion
piqué with clove. Poach thick-sliced bacon and local sausages. Poach
turned potatoes, turned carrots, turned turnips, leeks, and cabbage in
broth. (If desired, add beans such as navy beans.) Reserve. Serve with
side of coarse sea salt, Dijon mustard, and gherkins.

pot roast
Sear chuck roast. Add mirepoix. Add stock. Simmer until fork-tender.
(If desired, thicken with roux.)

Meats
&
Poultry

poulet basquaise [poo-LAY bah-skez]
French origin. Sauté chicken pieces. Sauté mirepoix. Make a roux.
Deglaze with white wine and reduce. Add sautéed red and green
peppers. Add chicken stock, tomatoes, herbs, salt, and pepper.
Simmer. (If desired, add sautéed bacon.)

poulet grillé en crapaudine [poo-lay GREE-yay ahn kra-poh-DEEN]
(see crapaudine)

Prince Orloff (see Orloff)

princesse; à la princesse [prehn-SES]
French origin. Roast, grill, or sauté meat. Garnish with asparagus tips.
Serve with demi-glace.

printanière; à la printanière [prehn-tahn-YAIR]
French origin. Roast, grill, or sauté meat. Garnish with spring
vegetables such as baby carrots, baby turnips, asparagus tips, pearl
onions, or any combination of these items.

Provençale; à la Provençale [proh-vahn-SAHL]
French origin. Roast, grill, or sauté meat. Garnish with tomato
concassée, peppers, eggplants, garlic, and olives.

ragoût [ra-GOO]
French origin. Sauté cubed meat until well-browned. Sauté mirepoix
or other vegetables. Add flour and make a brown roux. Deglaze with
dark brandy, water, or brown stock. Add brown stock and herbs. Salt
and pepper to taste. Simmer until meat is fork-tender.

ragu; ragù [rah-GOO]
Italian origin. Sauté mirepoix. Add ground meat such as beef, lamb or
pork. Add tomatoes and herbs. Salt and pepper to taste. Simmer.

raw kibbee (see kibbeh)

red flannel hash (see corned beef hash)

red-cooked pork
Chinese origin. Sauté scallions, garlic, and ginger. Add chicken stock,
dark soy sauce, rice wine, brown sugar, star anise, and other Chinese
spices. (If desired, add red food coloring.) Add pork shoulder. Simmer
until fork-tender. Serve with white rice.

Meats
&
Poultry

ropa vieja [roh-pah VYAY-hah]
Carribean origin. Regional variations. Braise beef flank steak with mirepoix until fork-tender. Shred. Sauté onions and peppers. Add shredded meat, braising liquid, tomatoes, garlic, cumin, herbs, salt, and pepper. Simmer. To finish, add sautéed red and yellow peppers, peas, and olives. Serve with yellow rice.

Rossini [roh-SEE-nee]
French origin. Sear filet mignon. Finish in oven to proper doneness. Serve with seared foie gras slice on top. Sauce with truffled demi-glace deglazed with Madeira wine. (If desired, add toast at the base.)

Salisbury steak
American origin. Mix ground beef with bread crumbs, onions, and seasonings. Broil. Serve with mashed potatoes and gravy.

salmis [SAL-mee]
French origin. Many variations. Slice game fowl meat such as pheasant or partridge. Place in dishware and sprinkle with diced truffles. (If desired, add diced foie gras.) Reduce stock. Add brandy and demi-glace. Sauce the meat and serve.

saltimbocca [sal-teem BOH-kuh] **alla Romana** (see veal saltimbocca)

satay; saté [sah-TAY]
Southeast Asian origin. Many regional variations. Similar to kebobs. Marinate beef or chicken strips with coarse peanut butter, soy sauce, coconut milk, ground cumin, ground coriander, curry paste, lime juice, sesame seeds, and sesame oil. Skewer and grill meat. Serve with or without dipping sauce.

sauté de veau [soh-TAY duh VOH]
French origin. Sauté veal cubes until browned. Reserve. Sauté onions. Deglaze with white wine. Add tomato sauce, stock, bouquet garni, and veal. (If desired, add vegetables.) Simmer until fork-tender.

shawarma [shah-WAHR-mah] (see doner-kebab)

shepherd's pie
British origin. Sauté mirepoix. Add ground lamb and tomato paste. Simmer. Salt and pepper to taste. (If desired, add peas.) Place in ovenproof dish. Pipe mashed potatoes on top and bake at 375°F.

Meats
&
Poultry

shish-kebab; shish kabob [SHISH kuh-bob]
Turkish origin. Skewer meat cubes such as lamb, pork, chicken, or beef with vegetables such as bell peppers and onions. Marinate with spices and herbs. Grill and serve.

sjömansbiffgryta [hreh-mahns-beef-GREET-ah]
Sailor stew. Swedish origin. Make a casserole with beef chuck, onions, potatoes, salt, pepper, and beer. Bake at 450°F for about 2 hours until meat is tender.

smothered steak (see Swiss steak)

snake and kiddy pie (see steak and kidney pie)

snake and pigmy pie (see steak and kidney pie)

steak and kidney pie
British origin. Simmer beef cubes and pork kidneys with beef broth, onions, Worcestershire, and parsley. Salt and pepper to taste. Thicken with cornstarch. Layer ovenproof dish with puff pastry or flaky pastry made with lard. Bake until pastry is golden.

steak and kidney pudding
British origin. Proceed as with steak and kidney pie. Line a pudding dish with flaky pastry made with lard. Pour in steak and kidney preparation. Cover with more pastry. Steam until pastry is done.

steak au poivre [oh PWAHV-ruh]
French origin. Encrust steak with cracked peppercorns. Sear and finish to doneness. Reserve. Sauté shallots. Flambé cognac. Deglaze with white wine and reduce. Add veal stock and reduce. Add cream and reduce. Add salt. Monter au beurre.

steak Diane
French origin. Sear beef tenderloin medallions and reserve. Sauté chopped shallots. Add mushrooms. Flambé with brandy. Add veal stock and reduce. Add Worcestershire and hot sauce. (If desired, add cream.) Return medallions to pan. (If desired, add chopped parsley.)

steak tartare [tar-TAR]
French origin. Shape and serve ground or hand-chopped beef tenderloin with raw egg yolk, minced shallots, parsley, capers, and gherkins. Serve with side of Worcestershire, Dijon mustard, tabasco-style sauce, salt, and pepper.

stroganoff [STROH-guh-nahf]
Russian origin. Sear sirloin or tenderloin cubes or strips. Sauté mushrooms and onions. Deglaze with white wine. Add nutmeg, salt, and pepper. Reduce and finish with sour cream. Do not boil after adding sour cream. Serve over rice pilaf.

stroganov (see stroganoff)

stromboli [strom-BOH-lee]
Italian origin. Make an Italian bread or pizza dough. Roll out flat. Top with a combination of meat (such as Italian sausage, ham or veal), vegetables (such as bell peppers, tomatoes or jalapeños), and cheese (such as ricotta, provolone or mozzarella). Season with salt, pepper, and fresh herbs. Roll into an oblong loaf and bake at 375°F.

sukiyaki [soo-kee-YAH-kee]
Japanese origin. Display shitake and enoki mushrooms, scallions, cabbage, tofu, and shirataki noodles. Make a sauce with soy sauce, sake, sugar, and mirin. Sear beef slices. Deglaze beef with sauce. Serve with a side of raw eggs for dipping.

Swedish meatballs
Swedish origin. Mix ground beef, ground pork, sautéed onions, bread crumbs, egg yolks, and nutmeg. Salt and pepper to taste. Beat until fluffy. Shape meatballs and sauté.

Swiss steak
American origin. Pound steak to tenderize. Dredge in flour. Sauté in bacon fat and reserve. Add onions, garlic, celery, tomato paste, tomatoes, herbs, Worcestershire, and beef broth. Add steak. Simmer until fork-tender.

tacos
Mexican origin. Make a filling with grilled beef, marinated pork, spicy chicken, or other meat. Add filling to tortillas. Sprinkle with chopped onions and cilantro. Serve with lime or key lime.

tajine [tah-ZHEEN]
North African origin. Soak tajine (clay dishware) in water overnight. Slow-simmer lamb neck or chicken legs in tajine dish with broth and North African spices. Add vegetables such as carrots, turnips, cabbage, potatoes, and olives. Salt and pepper to taste. Finish cooking.

tandoori chicken
Indian origin. Dry-rub chicken pieces with red chili powder, cumin, coriander, and garam masala. Marinate in yogurt, lime, and white vinegar. Pat-dry. Grill or roast in tandoor oven.

Tetrazzini [te-trah-ZEE-nee]
American origin (Southern). Poach chicken pieces in broth. Simmer. Make a roux by starting with a velouté and adding cream. Finish with salt, pepper, lemon juice, and nutmeg. Mix with sautéed mushrooms and spaghetti. Pour into ovenproof dish. Sprinkle with Parmigiano-Reggiano and bake au gratin.

Texas chili
American origin (Texas). Make a paste with toasted and blanched Guarillo chilies, cumin, salt, pepper, and water. Sear beef cubes, onions, and garlic. Deglaze with stock. Add chili paste and stock. Simmer. Finish with brown sugar and vinegar.

tournedos Rossini [toor-NEH-doh roh-SEE-nee] (see Rossini)

turkey Tetrazzini [te-trah-ZEE-nee] (see tetrazzini)

veal Marsala
Italian origin. Dredge veal scallopine in flour. Sauté. Salt and pepper to taste. Reserve. Deglaze with Marsala wine and reduce. Monter au beurre. Return veal to pan.

veal Orloff (see Orloff)

veal parmigiana [pahr-mee-ZHAN-nah]
Italian-American origin. Dredge veal in flour, then eggs, and then Parmigiano-Reggiano bread crumb mix. Sear veal. In ovenproof dish, layer veal, tomato sauce, Parmigiano-Reggiano, and mozzarella. Top with Parmigiano-Reggiano and bake au gratin.

veal piccata [pee-KAH-tuh]
Italian-American origin. Salt, pepper, and flour scallopine. Sear in butter. Reserve. Sauté minced shallots. Add capers. Deglaze with white wine. Add chicken stock and reduce. (If desired, monter au beurre.) Finish sauce with chopped fresh parsley and lemon juice. Return scallopine to pan.

veal saltimbocca [sal-teem-BOH-kuh]
Italian origin. Similar to involtini. Roll veal scallopine with prosciutto and mozzarella. Salt and pepper to taste. Secure with toothpicks. Sauté and reserve. Sauté shallots. Deglaze with white wine. Add stock and reduce. Monter au beurre.

veal sauté (see sauté de veau)

veal scallopine [skal-uh-PEE-neh]
Italian origin. Dredge veal scallopine in flour. Sauté. Salt and pepper to taste.

vendaloo [VIHN-dah-loo] (see vindaloo)

Véronique [vay-roh-NEEK]
French origin. Pound chicken breasts. Toss chicken with oil, salt, and pepper. (If desired, add fresh tarragon.) Sauté chicken and reserve. Sauté shallots and white grapes. Deglaze with wine and reduce. Thicken with cream.

vindaloo [VIHN-dah-loo]
Indian origin (Southwest). Process garlic, ginger, curry powder, mustard seeds, cumin, cardamom, cloves, cayenne pepper, white-wine vinegar, and olive oil. Salt and pepper to taste. Marinate pork or chicken. Roast or braise until tender. (If desired, braise with onions and tomatoes.) Finish with chopped cilantro.

vitello tonnato [vee-TEL-oh tuh-NAH-toh]
Italian origin. Poach lean veal roast meat with mirepoix until meat is tender. Reserve and chill. Slice thin. Make a blended sauce with canned tuna, anchovies, capers, extra virgin olive oil, and lemon juice. Fold in mayonnaise. Spread tuna sauce on veal slices and marinate overnight. Serve chilled.

waterzoi [VAH-ter-zoh-ee]
Belgian origin. Place chicken pieces in casserole. Top with julienned celery, chopped parsley, and leeks. Add consommé. Simmer.

Wiener Schnitzel; Wienerschnitzel [VEE-ner SHNIT-suhl]
Austrian/German origin. Similar to milanesas. Dredge scallopine in flour, then eggs, and then bread crumbs. Salt and pepper to taste. Sauté. Finish with a drizzle of lemon juice and fresh parsley.

Meats
&
Poultry

zingara; à la zingara [zin-GAH-rah]
   French origin. Sauté meat and reserve. Sauce with zingara sauce.

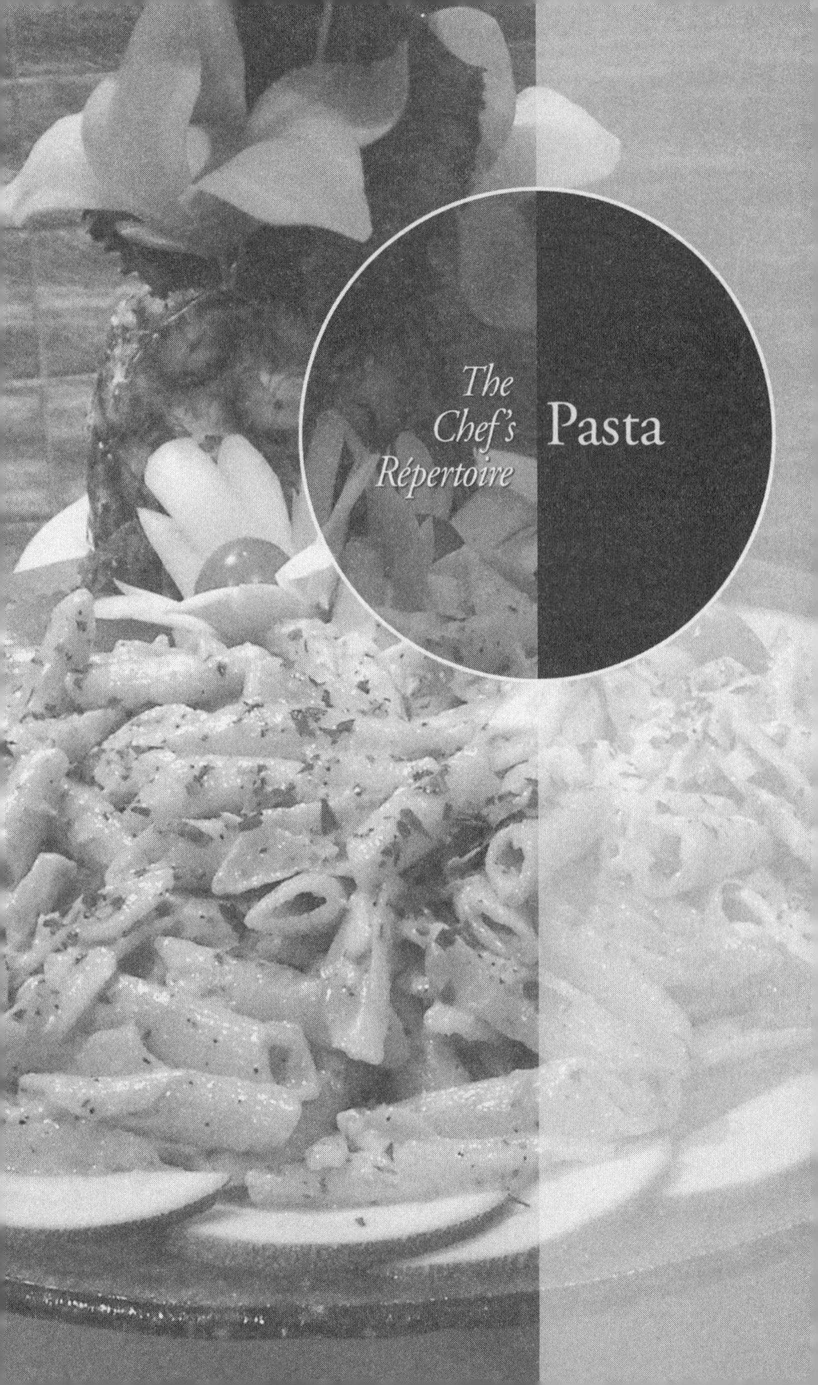
The Chef's Répertoire
Pasta

aglio e olio [AH-lyoh eh OH-lee-YOH]
Garlic and oil. Italian origin. Sauté chopped garlic in olive oil. Salt and pepper to taste. Toss with pasta al dente. Drizzle with olive oil.

agnolotti [ah-nyoh-LAH-tee]
Italian origin. Start with pasta dough. Roll out thin rectangle. Trim outer edges. Moisten surface. Pipe equal-sized dollops of filling such as cheese, ground meat, vegetables, or a combination of these items at 1½ inch intervals from the long edge. Pull top edge up and over fillings. Press and seal between each dollop of filling. Cut with pasta cutter. Poach in salt water.

Alfredo [al-FRAY-doh]
Italian origin. Cook fettuccine al dente. Make a smooth paste with room temperature butter and grated Parmigiano-Reggiano. Toss with fettuccine. Variation: Make an Alfredo sauce by adding cream, garlic, and Parmigiano-Reggiano to make a roux. (If desired, add chopped parsley, garlic, shrimp, or chicken.)

amatriciana [ah-MAH-tree-chee-AH-nah]
Sauté diced pancetta or guanciale with chili peppers. Deglaze with white wine. Add peeled, sliced tomatoes, salt, and pepper. Toss al dente pasta in sauce. Top with freshly grated Pecorino-Romano.

arrabiata [A-ruh-BYAHT-ah]
Italian origin. Traditionally served with penne. Start with red wine tomato sauce. Reinforce with fresh basil and chili peppers. Toss with al dente pasta. Garnish with fresh chopped parsley.

Bolognese; alla Bolognese [boh-luh-NYAY-zay]
Italian origin (Bologna). Sauté onions, garlic, and bacon. Add ground beef and tomato paste. Deglaze with red wine. (If desired, add tomato sauce.) Salt and pepper to taste. Simmer 2 hours.

Bolonaise [boh-luh-nez] (see Bolognese)

Bolonese [boh-luh-neez] (see Bolognese)

cacio e pepe [KAH-chee-yoh eh PEH-peh]
Cheese and pepper. Italian origin (Rome). Mix grated Pecorino-Romano and a suitable quantity of black pepper. Toss with al dente pasta. Serve immediately.

cannelloni [ka-ne-LOHN-ee]
Italian origin. Similar to manicotti. Pipe cheese, meat, and/or vegetable stuffing inside each cannelloni tube. Place cannelloni side by side in ovenproof dish and cover with tomato sauce and cheese. Bake.

cappelletti [ka-pe-LET-ee]
Italian origin. Make pasta dough. Roll sheet paper-thin. Cut 4-inch rounds. Make filling of ricotta, beef, spinach, or sausage. Pipe in filling. Egg-wash around filling. Fold in half over filling. Fold back around your finger, stick corners together and bend like a tortellini. Dust with flour and reserve. Boil like fresh pasta. Serve with tomato-based sauce, grated cheese, or pesto.

carbonara [kahr-boh-NAH-rah]
Cook spaghetti al dente. Toss with grated Parmigiano-Reggiano or Pecorino-Romano, raw egg yolks, fried pancetta or guanciale, and black pepper. (If desired, add salt and garlic.)

catizone [ka-ti-ZOHN-eh]
Sauté shrimp and scallops. Reserve. Sauté garlic, basil, and fennel. Add to shrimp and scallops. Toss with al dente linguine. Salt and pepper to taste. Add Parmigiano-Reggiano.

checca; alla checca [CHAY-kah]
Italian origin. Cook pasta al dente. Add diced skinless and seeded tomatoes, mozzarella, garlic, fresh arugula, basil, extra-virgin olive oil, salt, and pepper. Let rest until pasta has "cooked" the vegetables. (If desired, add Parmesan.)

chow fun [chow foon]
Chinese origin. American variations. Stir-fry meat such as chicken, pork, beef, or duck. Reserve. Stir-fry vegetables such as carrots, peppers, mushrooms. Add Chinese ho fun (wide rice) noodles, soy sauce, and oyster sauce thickened with cornstarch. Serve immediately.

chow mein [chow MAYN]
Chinese origin. American variations. Stir-fry chicken, pork, beef, or duck meat. Reserve. Stir-fry Asian-cut carrots, peppers, water chestnuts, bamboo shoots, and mushrooms. Add fried Chinese egg noodles, soy sauce, and oyster sauce thickened with cornstarch. Serve immediately.

cipolla; alla cipolla [chee-POL-lah]
With onions. Italian origin. Sauté onions and caramelize slightly.
Deglaze with white wine. Add stock. Salt and pepper to taste. Toss
with al dente pasta. Sprinkle with Parmigiano-Reggiano and drizzle
with extra-virgin olive oil.

con la ricotta [kohn lah ree-KOH-tah]
Italian origin (Sicily). Toss al dente pasta with fresh ricotta cheese. Salt
and pepper to taste. (If desired, add tomato sauce and rosemary.)

di bosco [dee BOH-skoh]
Italian origin. Sauté wild mushrooms, garlic, and herbs. Toss with
al dente pasta. Sprinkle with Parmigiano-Reggiano and drizzle with
extra-virgin olive oil.

di ricotta [dee ree-KOH-tah] (see con la ricotta)

Fra Diavolo [frah DYAH-voh-loh]
Italian origin. Sauté onions, peppers, and garlic. Add peeled and
seeded tomatoes, tomato paste, and chili peppers. Salt to taste.
Simmer. Serve with al dente pasta or seafood.

frutti de mare [FROO-tee day MAH-ray]
Fruits of the sea. Italian origin. Sauté scallops, clams, mussels,
calamari, and shrimp. Deglaze with white wine. Add tomato sauce,
garlic, and herbs. Toss with al dente pasta. Sprinkle with Parmigiano-
Reggiano and drizzle with extra-virgin olive oil.

funghi; ai funghi [igh FOON-gee]
With mushrooms. Italian origin. Sauté wild mushrooms, garlic, and
herbs. Toss with al dente pasta. Sprinkle with Parmigiano-Reggiano
and drizzle with extra-virgin olive oil.

Genoese; alla Genoese [jen-oh-EEZ]
Italian origin. Toss al dente pasta with pesto alla Genoese.

Genovese [jen-oh-VEEZ] (see Genoese)

gnocchi [NYOH-kee]
Italian origin. Mash one mealy potato. Add 1 egg yolk, 2 oz flour,
salt, and pepper. Knead. Roll into a long tube. Cut into 1-inch
pieces. Poach in salted water. Sauté or add to tomato sauce and
Parmigiano-Reggiano and bake au gratin.

Pasta

gnocchi di ricotta [NYOH-kee dee ree-KOH-tah]
Italian origin. Mix together 3 cups flour, 2 eggs, ½ cup Parmesan, and 1½ lb of ricotta cheese. Knead. Roll into a long tube. Cut into 1-inch pieces. Poach in salted water. Sauté or add to tomato sauce and Parmigiano-Reggiano and bake au gratin.

gorgonzola; alla gorgonzola [gor-gun-ZOH-lah]
Italian origin. Melt gorgonzola with cream and butter. Salt and pepper to taste. Do not overheat.

gricia [GREE-chee-ah]
Italian origin (Rome). Sauté guanciale. Do not brown. Deglaze with pasta cooking water. Toss in al dente pasta. Add grated Pecorino-Romano and freshly ground pepper.

hotsy pasta
Make a paste of garlic, extra-virgin olive oil, and anchovies. Sauté tomatoes, olives, capers, oregano, and red-pepper flakes. Mix in the paste. Simmer and reduce. Serve with al dente pasta.

kugel [KOO-guhl]
Jewish origin. Both sweet and savory variations. Make a pudding of potatoes or egg noodles, chopped vegetables or fruits, cottage or cream cheese, and a sweet or savory egg batter. Bake au gratin.

lasagna [luh-ZAHN-yuh]
Italian origin. Start with sheets of pasta dough. Layer pasta sheets, ricotta cheese, and Bolognese or tomato sauce in an ovenproof dish. (If desired, add béchamel or vegetables.) Top with cheese or béchamel. Bake au gratin.

limone; al limone [lee-MOH-neh]
Italian origin. Julienne lemon zest and add cream. Reduce. Toss in al dente pasta. Add butter, lemon juice, garlic, and chopped parsley. Salt and pepper to taste. Sprinkle with Parmigiano-Reggiano and drizzle with extra-virgin olive oil.

lo mein [loh MAYN]
Chinese origin. Many variations. Stir-fry chicken, pork, beef, or duck meat. Reserve. Stir-fry Asian-cut carrots, peppers, and mushrooms. Add Chinese egg noodles, soy sauce, and oyster sauce thickened with cornstarch. Serve immediately.

Pasta

macaroni and cheese
American origin. Mix al dente macaroni with thin sharp cheddar béchamel. Salt and pepper to taste. Bake au gratin.

manicotti [man-uh-KOT-tee]
Italian origin. Similar to cannelloni. Pipe cheese, meat, and/or vegetable stuffing inside each manicotti tube. Place manicotti side by side in ovenproof dish and cover with tomato sauce and cheese. Bake.

marinara
1. Italian origin. Quick-sauté garlic, Mediterranean herbs, and ripe tomatoes in olive oil. Add clams, mussels, and shrimp. Salt and pepper to taste. (If desired, add sugar for acidity correction.)
2. American origin. Start with tomato sauce. Reinforce with chopped garlic, fresh basil, and parsley. (If desired, add cayenne pepper or chilies.)

Napoletana [nah-poh-lee-TAH-nah] (see napolitana)

Napolitana; alla Napolitana [nah-poh-lee-TAH-nah]
Italian origin (Naples). Sauté garlic and onions. (If desired, add sweet peppers.) Deglaze with white wine. Add tomatoes, salt, and pepper. Simmer. Toss with al dente pasta. Add fresh basil. Sprinkle with Parmigiano-Reggiano and drizzle with extra-virgin olive oil.

noci; alle noci [NOH-chee]
With walnuts. Italian origin. Sauté garlic with bread crumbs, walnuts, pepper flakes, salt, and pepper. Add al dente pasta and toss. Sprinkle with Parmigiano-Reggiano and drizzle with extra-virgin olive oil.

norma; alla norma
Sauté diced eggplants in olive oil and garlic and reserve. Sauté peeled tomatoes and reserve. Toss al dente pasta with 1 cup of water, fresh basil, salt and pepper, ricotta salata, sautéed eggplants, and sautéed tomatoes.

omelet Napoletana [nah-poh-lee-TAH-nah]
Italian origin. Cook spaghetti. Sauté in butter. Add beaten eggs, milk, nutmeg, ham, mozzarella, salt, and pepper. Make into an omelet.

pad Thai [pad tigh]
Thai origin. Many variations. Stir-fry eggs, vegetables such as bean sprouts, and shrimp, chicken, or tofu. Add rice noodles. Season with soy sauce, fish sauce, chili peppers, lime, and tamarind. Add peanuts and fresh cilantro. Serve immediately.

panna; alla panna [PA-nah]
With cream. Italian origin. Toss al dente pasta with reduced cream, grated Parmigiano-Reggiano, salt, and pepper. (If desired, add white truffles and shredded prosciutto.)

pasta dough
Italian origin. Mix 3 cups flour, 4 eggs, a drizzle of olive oil, and salt to taste. Roll sheet paper-thin. Cut into desired shapes.

pasta e fagioli [PAH-stah eh faj-YOH-lee]
Pasta and beans. Italian origin. Sauté onions, pancetta, and garlic. Add cooked kidney beans, peeled and seeded tomatoes, and broth. Simmer. Add al dente macaroni. Salt and pepper to taste. Sprinkle with Parmigiano-Reggiano and drizzle with extra-virgin olive oil. Serve immediately.

pastitsio [pah-STEET-see-oh]
Greek origin. In ovenproof dish, layer tubular pasta with Bolongese or other meat-based sauce. Top with a nutmeg-flavored béchamel, Mornay, or egg-based custard. Sprinkle with cinnamon and cheese. Bake au gratin.

pesto; al pesto
Cook pasta al dente. Toss pasta with pesto sauce of fresh basil, Parmesan, pine nuts, garlic, olive oil, salt, and pepper. Sprinkle with Parmigiano-Reggiano and drizzle with extra-virgin olive oil.

pesto alla Calabrese [ka-lah-BRAY-zay]
Italian origin (Calabria). Process skinless grilled bell peppers, garlic, toasted pine nuts, Parmigiano-Reggiano, and basil. Monter with olive oil. Salt and pepper to taste.

pesto alla Genoese [jen-oh-EEZ]
Italian origin (Genoa). Process garlic, toasted pine nuts, Parmigiano-Reggiano, and basil. Whisk in olive oil. Salt and pepper to taste.

pesto alla Genovese [jen-oh-VEEZ] (see pesto alla Genoese)

pesto alla Siciliana [SEE-cheel-yah-nah]
Italian origin (Sicily). Process garlic, skinless and seeded tomatoes, Parmigiano-Reggiano, and basil. Monter with olive oil. Salt and pepper to taste.

pesto alla Trapanese [TRA-pah-NAY-zay]
Italian origin (Trapani). Process garlic, basil, and toasted almonds. Monter with olive oil. Add chopped, seedless, skinless tomatoes. Salt and pepper to taste.

pesto rosso [ROH-soh]
Italian origin. Process sun-dried tomatoes, extra-virgin olive oil, black olives, garlic, fines herbes, salt, and pepper.

piselli [pee-SEL-ee]
Italian origin. Sauté onions. Add marinara, fresh peas, salt, and pepper. Toss with al dente pasta. Sprinkle with Parmigiano-Reggiano and drizzle with extra-virgin olive oil.

pomarola [pohm-ah-ROHL-ah]
Italian origin. Sauté mirepoix. Add extra-virgin olive oil, chili peppers, skinless and seeded plum tomatoes, sugar, and garlic. Salt and pepper to taste. Simmer. Add fresh basil. Process. Serve immediately or preserve.

primavera [pree-muh-VAIR-uh]
Italian-American origin. Sauté or roast vegetables such as zucchini, carrots, peppers, broccoli, and asparagus. Toss with al dente pasta, garlic, and herbs. Sprinkle with Parmigiano-Reggiano and drizzle with extra-virgin olive oil.

pummarola [pum-ah-ROHL-ah] (see pomarola)

puttanesca; alla puttanesca [poo-tah-NEZ-kah]
Start with tomato sauce (pomarola). Add anchovies, capers, garlic, chili peppers, and black olives. Simmer for 30 minutes. Salt and pepper to taste.

ragu Bolognese (see Bolognese)

ravioli [ra-VYOH-lee]
Italian origin. Make pasta dough. Roll sheet paper-thin. Egg-wash half of the surface. Make filling of ricotta, beef, spinach, sausage, or any combination of these items. Pipe dollops of filling 2 inches apart on half the sheet. Fold the other half sheet on top of the fillings. Press out air pockets and seal in fillings. Cut into squares. Dust with flour and reserve. Boil like fresh pasta. Serve with tomato-based sauce, grated cheese, or pesto.

ravioli [ra-VYOH-lee] **dough**
Italian origin. Make dough from 1 lb flour, 2 eggs, salt, and 1 oz butter.

red pesto sauce (see pesto rosso)

Romana; alla Romana
Italian origin (Rome). Sauté guanciale. Do not brown. Deglaze with pasta cooking water. Toss in al dente pasta. Add grated Pecorino-Romano and freshly ground pepper.

salsa alla marinara (see marinara)

salsa cruda
Brunoise seeded tomatoes, onions, and serrano chilies. Add chopped fresh cilantro. Salt to taste.

salsa marinara (see marinara)

scampi
Italian origin. Sauté langoustine or Norway lobster with garlic. Salt and pepper to taste. Deglaze with dry vermouth. Add lemon juice and chopped parsley. Serve over al dente pasta. Variation: Use jumbo shrimp.

scoglio; allo scoglio [SKOL-yoh]
With shellfish. Italian origin. Sauté scallops, clams, mussels, calamari, and shrimp. Deglaze with white wine. Add tomato sauce, garlic, and herbs. Toss with al dente pasta. Sprinkle with Parmigiano-Reggiano and drizzle with extra-virgin olive oil.

Shanghai noodles
Stir-fry chopped ginger, garlic, and chili peppers. Add onions and ground beef. Deglaze with broth, soy sauce, and hoisin. Add Chinese egg noodles. Serve immediately.

Sichwan [SISH-wahn] **noodles; Sichuan noodles** (see Szechuan noodles)

Siciliana; alla Siciliana [SEE-cheel-yah-nah]
Italian origin (Sicily). Many variations. Roast eggplants until tender. Make a sauce of skinless, seeded tomatoes, garlic, and cooked eggplant. Add capers, black olives, and anchovies. Toss with al dente pasta. Sprinkle with Parmigiano-Reggiano and drizzle with extra-virgin olive oil.

Pasta

Singapore noodles
American origin. Stir-fry vegetables such as cabbage, shredded carrots, and shiitake mushrooms. (If desired, add shrimp or chicken.) Add rice vermicelli, curry powder, and soy sauce. Serve immediately.

spaetzle; spatzle [SHPETS-luh]
Eastern European origin. Make a slightly liquid batter with 8 oz flour, 2 eggs, salt and pepper, and water. Pour batter through colander into boiling salted water. Shock in ice water. Sauté.

sugo finto [SOO-goh FEEN-toh]
Fake sauce. Italian origin. Sauté onions, garlic, carrots, and celery. Add pancetta. Deglaze with white wine. Add skinless, seeded tomatoes. Simmer. Salt and pepper to taste. Serve with al dente pasta. Sprinkle with Parmesan and drizzle with extra-virgin olive oil.

Szechuan [SESH-wahn] **noodles; Szechwan noodles**
Stir-fry chopped ginger and garlic. Deglaze with teriyaki sauce, lime juice, and chili sauce. Add Chinese egg noodles. Serve immediately.

Tetrazzini [te-trah-ZEE-nee]
American origin (Southern). Start with leftover chicken or turkey. Mix with sautéed mushrooms, spaghetti, dry sherry, and béchamel. Salt and pepper to taste. Sprinkle with Parmesan and bake au gratin.

tordelli [tor-DEL-ee]
Italian origin. Make pasta dough. Roll sheet to paper-thin. Egg-wash half the surface. Make filling with ground beef, ground pork, Parmigiano-Reggiano, Tuscan pecorino, and greens. Pipe dollops of filling 2 inches apart on half the sheet. Fold the other half sheet on top of the fillings. Press out air pockets and seal in fillings. Cut into squares. Dust with flour and reserve. Boil like fresh pasta. Serve with tomato-based ground beef or pork sauce.

tortellini [tor-te-LEE-nee]
Italian origin. Make pasta dough. Roll sheet paper-thin. Cut into 4-inch rounds. Make filling from ricotta, beef, spinach, sausage, or any combination of these items. Pipe filling into each round. Egg-wash around the filling. Fold each round in half to cover filling. Then fold dough back around your finger, sticking corners together. Dust with flour and reserve. Boil like fresh pasta. Serve with tomato-based sauce, grated cheese, or pesto.

Trapanese [TRA-pah-NAY-zay] (see pesto alla Trapanese)

verde; al verde [VAIR-deh]
   Italian origin. Process garlic, scallions, fresh basil, and parsley. Add olives, capers, lemon juice, chili peppers, and Parmigiano-Reggiano. Salt and pepper to taste. Process. Monter with extra-virgin olive oil. Toss with al dente pasta.

vodka
   Italian origin. Sauté onions and garlic. Add fresh, skinless, seeded, chopped tomatoes, vodka, and chili peppers. Simmer. Add heavy cream and simmer. Serve over al dente pasta.

Pasta

The Chef's Répertoire Salads

baladi [BAH-lah-dee]
Egyptian origin. Tomatoes, cucumbers, onions, green chili peppers, mint, and Italian parsley. Serve with olive oil and lemon dressing.

Caesar
Mexican origin. American adaptaion. Toss romaine hearts with croutons and anchovy filets. Toss with Caesar dressing. Sprinkle with freshly grated Parmigiano-Reggiano and drizzle with olive oil. (If desired, add cherry or grape tomatoes, olives, chicken, or salmon.)

Caprese [kah-PRAY-zay]
Italian origin (Campania). Sliced tomatoes, sliced mozzarella, and fresh basil. Season with salt, pepper, and olive oil. (If desired, add chopped garlic.)

celery rémoulade [ray-muh-LAHD]
French origin. Grate or julienne celery root. Mix with mayonnaise. Serve cold.

celery victor
American origin (San Francisco). Poach celery hearts in veal or chicken stock and chill. Salt and pepper to taste. (If desired, top with anchovies.) Serve with a white wine vinegar and extra-virgin olive oil vinaigrette.

chef
American origin. Regional variations. Lettuce, hard-boiled eggs, cubes of cooked ham, turkey, or chicken, and hard cheese.

cobb
American origin. Lettuce, tomatoes, crisp bacon bits, chicken breast, hard-boiled eggs, avocado, Roquefort, chives, and baby corn.

coleslaw; cole slaw
1. Shredded white cabbage or jícama. (If desired, add shredded carrots.) Toss with mayonnaise.
2. Sliced green cabbage and thinly diced green pepper. (If desired, add grated carrots.) Season with grated onions, apple cider vinegar, sugar, and celery seeds. (If desired, add ketchup or barbecue sauce.)

crab Louie; crab Louis [LOO-ee]
American origin (West Coast). Lettuce, Dungeness crab meat, cucumbers, tomatoes, and green onions. Dust top of salad with paprika. Garnish with fresh chives. Serve with Louis dressing.

fattoush [fah-TOOSH]
Eastern Mediterranean origin. A mix of radishes, tomatoes, lettuce, cucumbers, onions, and peppers. Season with fresh mint, parsley, olive oil, salt, and lemon juice. Toss with stale, toasted, or fried pita bread.

garden
American origin. Iceberg or romaine with a combination of tomatoes, carrots, onions, cucumbers, olives, mushrooms, peppers, broccoli, celery, cheese, hard-boiled eggs, or croutons.

German potato
German origin. Many variations. Sliced potatoes, cooked and diced bacon, sautéed onions, and chopped celery. Season with bacon fat, salt, pepper, sugar, mustard, and chives. Serve warm.

Greek
Greek-American origin. Some variations. Tomatoes, cucumbers, onions, feta, kalamata olives, and oregano. (If desired, add iceberg lettuce and peppers.) Serve with extra-virgin olive oil vinaigrette.

insalata mista [ihn-sah-LAH-tah MIS-tah]
Mixed salad. Italian origin. Many variations. Bibb lettuce, radicchio, carrots, and cucumbers. Served with lemon juice and extra-virgin olive oil dressing.

kimchi [KIM-chee]
Korean origin. Many varations. Soak white cabbage strips in salted water until soft. Mix grated garlic, ginger, green onions, and daikon with fish sauce, chili powder, sugar, and rice vinegar. Mix in cabbage strips. Pickle for two days.

macédoine [mah-say-DWAHN]
French origin. Steam diced carrots, green beans, and potatoes. Steam green peas. Combine vegetables. Bind with mayonnaise. Serve chilled.

misickquatash [mi-SIK-kwuh-tahsh]
Native American origin. Boiled whole kernels of corn.

Niçoise [nee-SWAHZ]
French origin (Nice). Quartered tomatoes, anchovies, niçoise olives, steamed green beans, steamed new potatoes, hard-boiled eggs, and fresh or canned tuna. (If desired, add capers, lettuce, onions, and peppers.) Served with garlic vinaigrette.

Salads

panzanella [pahn-zah-NEL-lah]
Italian origin. Dice stale Tuscan bread. Add fresh tomatoes and basil.
Toss with vinaigrette. (If desired, add capers, anchovies, onions,
peppers, garlic, cucumbers, tuna, or hard-boiled eggs.)

salade verte [sah-LAHD VAIRT]
Green salad. French origin. Use Boston lettuce, romaine, escarole,
bibb, or a combination. Add fresh herbs such as tarragon or chervil.
(If desired, add garlic.) Serve with vinaigrette.

succotash [SUH-kuh-tash]
Native American origin. Corn kernels and garbanzo, lima, red kidney,
or black beans. (If desired, add raw tomatoes, onions, and peppers.)
Serve hot or cold.

tabbouleh [tuh-BOO-lee]
Middle-Eastern origin. Finely chopped parsley, bulgur, mint, and
diced tomatoes. Season with lemon juice, olive oil, salt, and pepper.

taboulé [ta-boo-LAY]
French version of tabbouleh. Fluffed couscous, tomatoes, onions, and
mint leaves. Seasoned with lemon juice and vinaigrette.

Waldorf
American origin (East Coast). Finely sliced green apples, celery, and
chopped walnuts. Toss with mayonnaise.

yam neua [yahm noo-AH]
Beef salad. Thai origin. Grill peppered beef tenderloin. Slice thin.
Marinate with lime juice, fish sauce, garlic, chilies, sugar, shallots,
cucumbers, cilantro, and mint.

The
Chef's
Répertoire

Sandwiches

bánh mì [ben me]
Vietnamese origin. Many variations. Carrot and daikon slaw, liver pâté, onion, cilantro, chili peppers, fish sauce, and chicken in a baguette. (If desired, add shredded pork skin, scrambled eggs, or tofu.)

barbecue; barbeque
Pulled barbecued pork, beef, or chicken on a bun.

Canadian chivito (see chivito)
Replace bacon with Canadian bacon.

cheese steak
American origin (Philadelphia). Pan-fry thinly sliced (chipped) steak. (If desired, add sautéed, thinly sliced onions and bell peppers.) Salt and pepper to taste. Melt cheese over steak. Place on Italian or French roll.

chivito
Uruguayan origin. Churrasco (grilled, thin-sliced steak), bacon, aioli or mayonnaise, mozzarella, tomatoes, green or black olives, and fried egg on a bun.

club; clubhouse
White meat turkey on three slices of toasted bread with lettuce, tomato, and mayonnaise. (If desired, add cheese and bacon.)

croque madame [krohk mah-DAHM]
French origin. Add a fried egg on top of a croque monsieur.

croque monsieur [krohk muh-SYER]
French origin. Toast white bread. Top with cooked ham, thick béchamel, and grated cheese. Broil. Serve hot.

Cuban sandwich
Roast pork, smoked ham, Swiss cheese, mustard, and pickles on Cuban bread. Press until golden.

grinder (see hero)

gyro [YEE-roh]
Greek origin. Shaved spit-roasted slices of spiced roasted lamb, beef, or chicken on a pita with yogurt-based sauce. Marinated beef or chicken may be used. (If desired, add onions, sweet peppers, and tomatoes.)

hero
Small loaf of Italian or French bread piled with meats and cheeses. (If desired, add peppers, lettuce, tomatoes, and pickles.) Also known as a grinder, hoagie, or submarine.

hoagie (see hero)

lobster roll
American origin (New England). Hot dog roll, mayonnaise or drawn butter, and cooked lobster meat. (If desired, add lettuce.)

Monte Cristo [MON-tee KRIHS-toh]
American origin. White bread, turkey, ham, and Swiss cheese. Dip entire sandwich in egg batter. Deep-fry. (If desired, sprinkle with confectioners' sugar.)

Monte Cubano [MON-tee KOO-bah-noh]
Cuban bread, mustard, aioli, pickles, smoked ham, turkey, Swiss cheese. Dip entirely in batter. Deep-fry or sauté in butter.

muffuletta; muffaletta [muh-fuh-let-uh]
American origin (New Orleans). Rustic Sicilian bread or focaccia, Genoa salami, mortadella, provolone, and olive salad (chopped green and black olives, capers, red peppers, parsley, garlic, and olive oil).

pan bagnat [pan ban-YAH]
French origin. Round French bread, tuna, tomatoes, onions, red and green peppers, black olives, hard-boiled eggs, anchovies, and a drizzle of olive oil.

panini [pah-NEE-nee]
Italian origin. Many variations. Ciabatta bread. Salami, ham, or other cured meats and cheeses. (If desired, add grilled vegetables.) Usually pressed or grilled and served hot.

pizza, Chicago style
American origin (Chicago). Some variations. Dissolve 1 package dry yeast into 1¼ cups warm water. Combine 2¾ cups flour, ½ cup cornmeal, 3 tablespoons olive oil, salt, and yeast mixture. Knead. Separate into workable balls. Allow to rise 2 hours at room temperature. Roll balls into 13-inch diameter circles. Transfer to deep-dish pizza pans. Top with tomato sauce, cheese, pizza toppings, and herbs. Bake on pizza stone in a 500°F oven for 20 minutes.

pizza, deep dish (see pizza, Chicago style)

pizza, Neapolitan style
Italian origin. Regional variations. Dissolve 1 teaspoon dry yeast into 3 cups warm water. Combine 9 cups of flour, salt, and yeast. Knead. Separate into workable balls. Let rise overnight in refrigerator. Let rise 2 hours at room temperature. Shape balls into 12-inch diameter circles. Keep thin. Top with tomato sauce, pizza toppings, cheese, and herbs. Bake on pizza stone in a 500°F oven for 20 minutes.

pizza, New York style (see pizza, Neapolitan style)

po' boy; po-boy; po boy
American origin (Louisiana). French bread, fried oysters, shrimp, crab, crawfish, catfish, hot sausage, or beef. (If desired, add mayonnaise, lettuce, tomato, pickle, onion, or mustard.)

Rachel
American origin. Rye bread, coleslaw, Swiss cheese, pastrami or turkey, Thousand Island dressing, and optional sweet pickle relish. Grill, toast, or sauté sandwich in butter.

Reuben [ROO-ben]
American origin. Rye bread, sauerkraut, Swiss cheese, corned beef or turkey. (If desired, add Thousand Island dressing or pickle relish.) Grill, toast, or sauté sandwich in butter.

sloppy Joe
Sauté onion, celery, jalapeño, bell pepper, and garlic. Add ground beef, tomato sauce, tabasco-style sauce, Worcestershire sauce, and ketchup. Cook until thick. Serve on buns.

submarine (see hero)

tacos
Mexican origin. Make a filling with grilled beef, marinated pork, spicy chicken, or other meat. Add filling to tortillas. Sprinkle with chopped onions and cilantro. Serve with lime or key lime.

The
Chef's Sides
Répertoire

à la grecque [GREK]
Simmer water, white wine, diced onions, garlic, lemon juice, vinegar, coriander seeds, fennel seeds, thyme, and bay leaf. Add vegetables such as whole mushrooms or fennel bulbs. Simmer until tender. Serve chilled.

à l'anglaise [ah lahn-GLEZ]
French origin. Boil in salted water.

à la Bourguignonne [boor-gee-NYUN]
French origin. Served with glacé à brun pearl onions, sautéed mushrooms, and sautéed bacon.

almondine (see amandine)

amandine [AH-mahn-deen]
With almonds. French origin. Garnish fish or vegetables with almonds.

Anna (see pommes Anna)

arroz à la Mexicana [ah-ROHS ah lah meh-hee-KAH-nuh]
Mexican rice. Mexican origin. Sauté onions. Add rice and toss in fat until translucent. Add 2:1 mixture of garlic, puréed tomatoes, carrots, chilies, peas, and chicken stock. Simmer until liquid has evaporated and rice is tender. Add chopped cilantro and lemon juice. Salt and pepper to taste.

arroz blanco [ah-ROHS BLAN-koh]
White rice. Mexican origin. Simmer 1 volume of white rice in 2 volumes of water.

arroz con pollo [ah-ROHS kohn POH-yoh]
Rice with chicken. Spanish/Latin American origin. Marinate chicken with oregano, cumin, white pepper, and vinegar. Sear chicken in annatto or olive oil. Make a sofrito with diced onions, peppers, garlic, and tomatoes. Add water, wine, tomato paste, salt, and pepper. (If desired, add saffron.) Simmer. Cook Valencia-style rice with annatto seeds and chicken fat. Add peas and pimientos.

arroz y frijoles [ah-ROHS ee free-HOH-lays]
Rice and beans. Combination of arroz blanco and frijoles.

artichokes barigoule [bah-ree-GOOL]
French origin (Provence). Sauté onions, mushrooms, and carrots in olive oil. Add artichoke hearts, bay leaf, garlic, and thyme. (If desired, add tomatoes.) Salt and pepper to taste. Add white wine. Cover and simmer. Finish by reducing the sauce.

artichokes Saint-Germain [san-zher-MEHN]
French origin. Artichoke bottoms filled with fresh green-pea purée.

barigoule [bah-ree-GOOL] (see artichokes barigoule)

bashed neeps
Scottish origin. Mashed turnips.

bibimbap [be-beem-bop]
Korean origin. Boil rice. Wilt spinach. Sauté bean sprouts. Sauté julienned zucchini. Stir-fry kosari. Sauté shitake mushrooms. Sauté ground beef and season with soy sauce, garlic, sugar, and peppers. Sauté julienned carrots. Prepare egg sunny-side up. To assemble, place rice in the middle of a large platter and display vegetables and meat around it. Place egg on top. Drizzle with sesame oil and chili oil. Serve immediately.

biryani [bee-ree-AH-nee]
Indian origin. Many regional variations. Sauté onions with marsala. Add vegetables such as cauliflower, green beans, potatoes, and chilies. Add meat such as chicken or lamb. Add saffron or turmeric, yogurt, and cilantro. Simmer. Cook basmati rice separately. Add rice to vegetables and meat. Cover and finish cooking.

blatjang [blud yung]
South African origin. Soak dried apricots and raisins. Slowly simmer apricots and raisins with onions, garlic, almonds, brown sugar, and spices such as cayenne pepper, coriander, and ginger. Reduce to consistency of chutney.

blooming onion; bloomin' onion
Make a batter with 1½ cups flour, ⅓ cup cornstarch, chopped garlic, paprika, salt, pepper, and 24 oz of beer. Place onions on a cutting board with the core down. Slice without cutting through. Pivot at 90° and continue slicing as onion "blooms." Dredge in flour, then in batter. Deep-fry until golden.

Boston baked beans
Rinse navy beans. Add water and simmer until beans are soft. Make a sauce with water, molasses, cloves, salt, and pepper. Add sauce and salt pork to beans. Bake slowly for 4 or 5 hours.

boulangère [boo-lahn-ZHAIR]
French origin. Roasted meat on top of pommes boulangère.

Sides

caponata [kap-oh-NAH-tah]
Italian origin (Sicily). Local variations. Steam or sauté eggplant. Sauté onions and celery. Add tomato concassée or pulp. Add eggplant, black olives, and capers. (If desired, add vinegar and sugar.) Let thicken. Salt and pepper to taste. Serve chilled.

caramelized onions
Sauté onions until translucent. Turn down heat and slow-cook until onions caramelize.

carrots Vichy [VEE-shee]
French origin. Slice carrots. Place in saucepan and barely cover with water, sugar, and butter. Bring to a boil and cook until water is evaporated.

casserole, vegetable
Many variations. Vegetables cooked in a Dutch oven or skillet. Sometimes covered with bread crumbs or cheese and baked au gratin.

celery victor
American origin (San Francisco). Poach celery hearts in veal or chicken stock and chill. Salt and pepper to taste. (If desired, top with anchovies.) Serve with a white-wine vinegar and extra-virgin olive oil vinaigrette.

chappit tatties
Scottish origin. Mashed potatoes with greens.

cholay [CHOH-lay]
Pakistani origin. Sauté onions with cumin seeds and red chilies. Add cooked chick peas, tomatoes, salt, and pepper. Simmer. Finish with fresh cilantro.

Clamart; à la Clamart [kla-MAHR]
French origin. Artichoke bottoms garnished with petits pois à la française and pommes château.

coleslaw; cole slaw
1. Shred white cabbage or jícama. (If desired, add shredded carrots.) Toss with mayonnaise.
2. Slice green cabbage and thinly dice green pepper. (If desired, add grated carrots.) Season with grated onions, apple-cider vinegar, sugar, and celery seeds. (If desired, add ketchup or barbecue sauce.)

collard greens miniera [mee-NYAIR-uh]
Brazilian origin. Sauté bacon. Add chiffonade of collard greens and wilt. Salt and pepper to taste.

congee [KAHN-jee]
Chinese origin. Asian variations. Start with sushi rice. Add water and simmer until soup becomes silky. Add soy sauce and pepper to taste. (If desired, add ginger, garlic, greens, tofu, and beans.)

Conti; à la Conti [KOHN-tee]
French origin. Lentil purée with sautéed bacon.

corn fritters
Make a batter with 2 egg yolks, 2 tablespoons flour, 1 tablespoon sugar, 2 beaten egg whites, and salt and pepper to taste. Add corn kernels to the mix. Sauté small amounts of batter to form fritters. Serve immediately.

corn mash (see corn pudding)

corn on the cob
Grill, steam, or boil whole corn. Serve immediately with butter, salt, and pepper.

corn pudding
American origin. Mix béchamel sauce with steamed corn. Bake au gratin.

country pudding (see corn pudding)

dal; dhal; dhall [DAHL]
Indian origin. Soak and boil chick peas, mung beans, lentils, black-eyed peas, or other beans. Pan-fry garam masala with onions. Add chopped tomatoes and yogurt. Add cooked beans. Sprinkle with cilantro.

dauphine [doh-FEEN] (see pommes dauphine)

Delmonico potatoes
American origin. Dice and blanch potatoes. Sauté in butter. Mix with béchamel sauce and cheddar cheese. Bake au gratin.

deviled potatoes
Halve potatoes. Bake covered with parchment paper, or steam. Scoop out the inside. Mix with butter, sour cream or mayonnaise, herbs, and salt and pepper to taste. Pipe mixture back into the potato halves. Serve immediately after baking.

Dieppoise [dee-uh-PWAHZ]
French origin. Whole mushroom tops, shrimp, and mussels.

Sides

dirty rice
American origin (Louisiana). Sauté thinly chopped bell peppers, onions, celery, and garlic in Cajun spices. Sauté ground meat. Add rice and stock. Simmer until cooked. (If desired, add chicken livers.)

doria
French origin. Sauté tournéed cucumbers in butter.

Dubarry; à la Dubarry [doo-BAIR-ee]
French origin. Cauliflower coated with Mornay sauce and served with pommes château.

duchesse potatoes (see pommes duchesse)

duxelles [dook-SEL]
French origin. Sauté chopped shallots and chopped mushrooms. (If desired, flambé with cognac.) Deglaze with white wine. Reduce until dry. Salt and pepper to taste.

eggplant parmigiana [pahr-mee-ZAHN-nah]
Italian origin. Cut thick rounds of eggplants. Dredge in flour, then eggs, and then bread crumbs. Salt and pepper to taste. Sauté in extra-virgin olive oil. In ovenproof dish, layer eggplant, oregano, mozzarella, and grated Parmigiano-Reggiano. Top with tomato sauce. Bake au gratin.

étuvée; à l'étuvée [ah lay-too-VAY]
French origin. Shallow poach vegetables such as peas or tournéed carrots with butter. Cook covered over low heat.

excelsior
French origin. Serve with braised lettuce and pommes fondantes.

farcis [fahr-SEE]
French origin (Provence). Stuff green and red peppers with a ground beef, pork, or lamb (or any combination), mushrooms, onions, potatoes, zucchini, garlic, herbes de Provence, salt, and pepper. Bake at 350°F.

flamande; à la flamande [flah-MAHND]
French origin. Braised cabbage, tournéed carrots and turnips, sautéed bacon, and pommes anglaise.

Florentine [FLOHR-uhn-teen]
French origin. Served with wilted spinach.

forestière; à la forestière [foh-res-TYAIR]
French origin. Sauté morels, bacon, and mashed potatoes.

French fries
Belgian origin. Cut potatoes into thick strips. Soak in water. Pat-dry.
Deep-fry in oil at 325ºF for 6 to 8 minutes until potatoes are soft and
limp. Remove fries and rest for 10 minutes to 1 hour. Bring oil to
350ºF and fry blanched potatoes again until golden brown. Salt and
pepper to taste. Serve immediately.

fried green tomatoes
American origin (Southern). Make a mix with 2 cups cornmeal,
½ cup flour, paprika, chopped parsley, and salt and pepper to taste.
Slice green tomatoes and dip in milk, then into mix. Pan-fry until
golden. Serve immediately.

fried rice
Chinese origin. Fully cook rice ahead. Scramble eggs in a wok and
reserve. Stir-fry scallions in sesame oil. Add rice, green peas, and Asian
cuisine by-products such as diced pork, chicken, or vegetables. (If
desired, add seasonings such as soy sauce and chili peppers.)

frijoles [free-HOH-lays]
Mexican origin. Rinse dried black beans. Sauté onions with jalapeño
peppers. Add beans and water. Simmer until beans are tender. Salt
and pepper to taste. Serve with sour cream and tortillas.

frijoles negros [free-HOH-lays NAY-grohs] (see frijoles)

glacé à blanc [glah-say ah BLAHNK]
Place pearl onions or tournéed vegetables such as carrots and zucchini in
sauce pan. Barely cover with water. Add butter, sugar, and pepper. Boil
until water is evaporated and onions or vegetables are slightly glazed.

glacé à brun [glah-say ah BROO]
Place pearl onions or tournéed vegetables such as carrots and zucchini
in sauce pan. Barely cover with water. Add butter, sugar, and pepper.
Boil until water evaporates. Caramelize until vegetables are slightly
brown.

gohan [GOH-hahn]
Japanese origin. Rinse short-grain rice 3 times. Boil 1 cup short-grain
rice with 1 cup cold water. Let rest.

Sides

gratin [gra-TEHN] (see gratinata)

gratinata [gra-tee-NAH-tuh]
Italian origin. Bake potatoes or vegetables in an ovenproof dish with sauce. Top with cheese and cook until top is brown.

gratin Dauphinois [gra-TEHN doh-FEEN-wah]
French origin (Dauphiné). Thinly slice potatoes with mandoline. Mix with chopped garlic, nutmeg, salt, and pepper. Layer in ovenproof dish. Barely cover with cream or half-and-half. Bake au gratin at 350°F until cream evaporates and potatoes are cooked and brown on top.

gumbo, green (see gumbo z'herbes)

gumbo z'herbes [GUHM-boh ZAIRB]
Gumbo with greens. American origin (Louisiana). Blanch assorted greens such as collard greens, mustard greens, spinach, watercress, Sorrel, and dandelions. Sauté onions with cayenne pepper and Cajun spices. Add flour and make a brown roux. Add bell peppers, celery, and blanched greens. Salt and pepper to taste. Add vegetable stock. (If desired, add ham hock.) Simmer for 2 hours.

Harvard beets
Parboil beets. Add vinegar, sugar, cornstarch, and salt to the cooking liquid. Bring back to a boil, thicken, and finish cooking.

hash browns
Peel and shred potatoes. Add diced onions. Salt and pepper to taste. Sauté. Press down in skillet or on griddle and slow-cook until tender and golden brown. Serve immediately.

hoppin' John
American origin (Southern). Sauté onions and celery. Add garlic and red pepper flakes. Add black-eyed peas. Simmer until peas are cooked. Serve with rice.

hoppy glop (see corn pudding)

imperiale [em-pee-ree-AL]
French origin. Foie gras slices, truffles, and mushrooms.

Japanese rice (see gohan)

Joinville [ZHWAHN-vee-uh]
French origin. Diced cooked mushrooms, truffles, and shrimp with Normande sauce.

kugel [KOO-guhl]
Jewish origin. Both sweet and savory variations. Make a pudding of potatoes or egg noodles, chopped vegetables or fruits, cottage or cream cheese, and a sweet or savory egg batter. Bake au gratin.

latke [LAHT-kuh]
Jewish origin. Similar to potato pancakes. Prepare a mixture of 2 lb grated potatoes, 1 lb grated onions, ½ cup flour, and 3 eggs. Salt and pepper to taste. Sauté pancakes and finish in oven.

leeks vinaigrette [vee-nuh-GRET]
French origin. Steam leeks until soft and tender. Chill. Serve with mustard vinaigrette.

Lorraine [loh-REN]
French origin. Braised red cabbage and pommes fondantes.

Lyonnaise [lee-uh-NEZ]
French origin. Parboil potatoes, then slice thick. Sauté. Add sautéed onions. Finish in oven.

maque choux [mahk SHOO]
American origin (Louisiana). Sauté onions, tasso, corn, and bell peppers. (If desired, add a scrambled mixture of beaten eggs and milk.) Add garlic, Cajun spices, and stock. Simmer. Serve immediately.

misickquatash [mi-SIK-kwuh-tahsh]
Native American origin. Boiled whole kernels of corn.

mousse, vegetable
Purée vegetables such as asparagus, carrots, and zucchini. Add 1 beaten egg per cup of vegetables. Pour in ramekins. Bake in bain-marie until firm.

Nemours [nuh-MOOR]
French origin. Green peas, tournéed carrots, and pommes duchesse.

Niçoise; à la Niçoise [nee-SWAHZ]
1. French origin. Tomato concassé, capers, and garlic used to sauce fish.
2. French origin. Tomato confite, sautéed French green beans, and pommes château served with meats or poultry.

Sides

onion rings
Slice whole onion into rings. Dip in fritter batter of 1⅓ cup flour, salt, pepper, 2 egg yolks, ¾ cup beer, and 2 slightly beaten egg whites. Deep-fry. Salt and pepper to taste. Serve immediately.

Orloff
French origin. Celery purée, stuffed lettuce leaves, tomato confite, and pommes château.

paillasson [PIGH-uh-sohn]
French origin. Similar to potato pancakes. Grate potatoes. Salt and pepper to taste. Shape into small pancakes. Sauté and finish in oven.

parisienne [pair-ee-ZYEN]
French origin. Braised lettuce with pommes parisienne.

paysanne [PAY-zahn]
French origin. Paysanne-cut carrots, turnips, and onions. Add pommes cocotte, sautéed bacon, and tournéed carrots.

peperonata [peh-peh-roh-NAH-tuh]
Italian origin. Many regional variations. Sauté red and green peppers with onions, garlic, salt, and pepper. (If desired, add skinless, seedless tomatoes.) Serve chilled, warm, or at room temperature.

Persian rice
Boil long-grain rice with cinnamon, cloves, cardamom, salt, and pepper. Keep firm. Sauté onions and saffron in clarified butter. Add cooked rice. (If desired, add dried apricots and raisins.) Press and cover. Bake until bottom of rice has made a crust.

petits farcis [puh-TEE fahr-SEE] (see farcis)

petits pois à la Française [puh-TEE pwah ah lah frahn-SEZ]
French origin. Sauté thinly diced onions. Add diced carrots, peas, lettuce chiffonade, butter, and enough water to cook. Salt and pepper to taste. Serve when peas are cooked.

pilaf [PEE-lahf] (see rice pilaf)

pilau; pilaw [PEE-lahw] (see rice pilau)

pipérade [pee-PAY-rahd]
French/Spanish origin (Basque region). Sauté onions, green peppers, and skinless, seedless tomatoes. (If desired, add garlic.) Add salt and Espelette pepper to taste. Serve warm or chilled.

poireaux vinaigrette [pwahr-OH vee-nuh-GRET] (see leeks vinaigrette)

pommes allumette [pumz al-loo-MET]
French origin. Cut thick julienned potatoes. Deep-fry. Salt and pepper to taste. Serve immediately.

pommes anglaise [pumz ahn-GLEZ]
French origin. Tourné potatoes 6 cm in length. Cook a l'anglaise. Salt and pepper to taste.

pommes Anna [pumz AHN-uh]
French origin. Thinly slice potatoes with mandoline. Place on bottom of skillet, forming a symmetrical design. Drench with clarified butter. Start on the stove, flip over, and finish in oven. Serve immediately.

pommes boulangère [pum boo-lahn-ZHAIR]
French origin. Thinly slice potatoes with mandoline. Salt and pepper. Layer in ovenproof dish with sautéed onions. Barely cover with chicken stock. Bake au gratin at 350°F until stock has evaporated and potatoes are cooked and brown on top.

pommes château [pum SHA-toh]
French origin. Tourné potatoes 7.5 cm in length. Blanch. Sauté in butter.

pommes [pum] **chips**
French origin. Slice potatoes as thin as possible with mandoline. Deep-fry.

pommes cocotte [pum koh-KAHT]
French origin. Tourné potatoes 5 cm in length. Blanch. Sauté in butter.

pommes croquettes [pum kroh-KET]
French origin. Many variations. Similar to fritters. Make a base with mashed potatoes, spices, and herbs. Shape into bite-sized cylinders or footballs. (If desired, dip in egg batter.) Roll in bread crumbs. Deep-fry.

pommes dauphine [pum doh-FEEN]
French origin. Force cooked potatoes through a ricer. Add ¼ cup flour to ⅓ cup hot water, butter, and nutmeg for each cup of riced potatoes. Proceed as with pâté à choux. Add 1 egg. Salt and pepper. Add riced potatoes. Mix well. Pipe croquettes directly into deep-fryer. Serve immediately.

pommes duchesse [pum doo-SHES]
French origin. Force cooked potatoes through a ricer. Add butter, salt, and pepper. (If desired, add egg yolks.) Pipe onto sheet pan. Bake until outside is slightly crusty and golden and inside is moist. Serve immediately.

pommes fondantes [pum fohn-DAHNT]
French origin. Tourné potatoes 9 cm in length. Place in roasting pan. Barely cover with white stock and then parchment paper. Bake until tender.

pommes frites [pum FREET] (see French fries)

pommes gaufrettes [pum goh-FRET]
French origin. Criss-cross cut potatoes with mandoline. Deep-fry.

pommes Lorette [pum loh-RET]
French origin. Make a pâté à choux. Add mashed potatoes. Pipe into deep-fryer until golden. Serve immediately.

pommes nature [pum nah-TYOOR] (see pommes anglaise)

pommes noisette [pum nwah-ZET]
French origin. Cut potatoes into round balls with melon baller. Blanch. Sauté with clarified butter. Finish in oven. Salt and pepper to taste.

pommes paille [pum PIGH]
French origin. Use a mandoline to julienne potatoes in long slices. Soak in ice water. Drain and dry well. Deep-fry to blanch. Then deep-fry again to brown. Salt and pepper to taste.

pommes parisienne [pum pair-ee-ZYEN]
French origin. Cut potatoes into round balls with melon baller. Blanch. Sauté with clarified butter. Finish with demi-glace. Salt and pepper to taste.

pommes pont-neuf [pum pon-NEUF]
French origin. Cut potatoes in thick batonnets. Deep-fry.

pommes rissolées [pum ree-soh-LAY]
French origin. Proceed as with pommes château, but brown more.

pommes Salardaise [pum sahr-duh-LEZ]
French origin (Southwest). Blanch potatoes. Sauté in duck fat and slow-cook until tender. Add salt, pepper, garlic, and parsley. (If desired, add truffles or sautéed porcini.)

pommes sautées [pum soh-TAY]
French origin. Cook potatoes robe de chambre. When tender, peel. Slice thick. Sauté in clarified butter. Salt and pepper to taste. Garnish with chopped parsley.

pommes soufflées [pum soo-FLAY]
French origin. Slice potatoes thin with mandoline. Deep-fry once to blanch. Deep-fry again to brown. Salt and pepper to taste.

pommes vapeur [pum va-PER]
French origin. Tourné potatoes 6 cm in length. Steam. Salt and pepper to taste.

posole [poh-SOH-leh]
Latin American origin. Make a chili paste with red Anaheim and jalapeño peppers. Reserve. Sauté onions and red bell peppers. Add parboiled hominy and chicken stock. Simmer until well-cooked. Salt and pepper to taste. Finish with lemon juice. Serve with rice and chili paste on the side.

potatoes au gratin [oh gra-TEHN]
American origin. Variation of gratin Dauphinois. Parboil potatoes. Slice and layer in an ovenproof dish. Add béchamel sauce with grated cheddar cheese. Bake au gratin.

potatoes Salardaise [sahr-duh-LEZ] (see pommes Salardaise)

pozole [poh-ZOH-leh] (see posole)

princesse [prehn-SES]
French origin. Artichoke bottoms with asparagus tips and pommes noisette.

printanière [prehn-tahn-YAIR]
French origin. Tourné carrots and turnips, glacé à brun pearl onions, French green beans, asparagus tips, and peas.

puddin' corn (see corn pudding)

purée
French origin. Peel and boil potatoes. Drain. Pass through ricer. Salt and pepper to taste.

purée Argenteuil [ahr-zhahn-TOY-eh]
French origin. Cook asparagus tips. Blend in food processor. Salt and pepper to taste.

purée Clamart [kla-MAHR]
French origin. Cook fresh green peas. Blend in food processor. Salt and pepper to taste.

purée Condé [KOHN-day]
French origin. Cook red beans. Blend in food processor. Salt and pepper to taste.

purée Conty [KOHN-tee]
French origin. Cook lentils. Blend in food processor. Salt and pepper to taste.

purée Crécy [KRAY-see]
French origin. Cook carrots and rice. Blend in food processor. Salt and pepper to taste.

purée Dubarry [doo-BAIR-ee]
French origin. Cook cauliflower. Blend in food processor. Salt and pepper to taste.

purée parmentier [pahr-MAHN-tyay]
French origin. Cook potatoes. Mash. Salt and pepper to taste.

purée Saint-Germain [san-zher-MEHN]
French origin. Cook fresh peas. Blend in food processor. Salt and pepper to taste.

purée soubise [soo-BEEZ]
French origin. Cook onions. Blend in food processor. Salt and pepper to taste.

purée Vichy [VEE-shee]
French origin. Cook carrots. Blend in food processor. Salt and pepper to taste.

rajas [RAH-hahs]
Mexican origin. Regional variations. Slice roasted, peeled green poblano chilies and reserve. Sauté onions and garlic. Add chilies and cream. Salt and pepper to taste. Simmer.

ratatouille [ra-tuh-TOO-ee]
French origin (Provence). Many variations. Dice eggplant, zucchini, red peppers, and onions. Sauté each vegetable separately. Gather in one pan. Add chopped, peeled, and seeded tomatoes. Add garlic and herbes de Provence. Salt and pepper to taste. Simmer 20 minutes.

Sides

refried beans
Mexican origin. Sauté onions. Add frijoles and mash coarsely. Add water if necessary. Salt and pepper to taste. Serve hot with queso fresco.

rice Creole
Make a rice pilaf. Add sautéed mushrooms, diced green peppers, and tomato concassée.

rice pilaf [PEE-lahf]
Sauté onions. Add 1 volume of uncooked rice. Toss in fat until translucent. Add 2 volumes of water or stock, bay leaves, salt, and pepper. Bring to a boil. Cover and transfer to oven. Bake 20 minutes. Fluff rice.

rice pilau [PEE-lahw] (see rice pilaf)

risi e bisi [REE-see eh BEE-see]
Italian origin. Sauté onions and pancetta until onions are translucent. Add chicken stock, Arborio rice, and white wine. Stir slowly to cook and release starch. Keep soft and creamy. Salt and pepper to taste. Add sautéed sugar snap peas and greens. Finish with butter and grated Parmigiano-Reggiano.

risotto alla piedmontese [ree-SOH-toh ah lah pyay-mahn-TAY-zay]
Italian origin. Sauté onions and wild mushrooms. (If desired, sauté Italian sausage or chicken livers.) Add chicken stock, Arborio rice, and white wine. Stir slowly to cook and release starch. Keep soft and creamy. Salt and pepper to taste. Finish with butter and grated Parmigiano-Reggiano.

risotto in bianco [ree-SOH-toh een bee-ANH-koh]
Italian origin. Sauté onions until translucent. Add chicken stock, Arborio rice, and white wine. Stir slowly to cook and release starch. Keep soft and creamy. Salt and pepper to taste. Finish with butter and grated Parmigiano-Reggiano.

risotto Milanese [ree-SOH-toh mee-lah-NAY-seh]
Italian origin (Milan). Sauté onions with saffron until translucent. Add chicken stock, Arborio rice, and white wine. Stir slowly to cook and release starch. Keep soft and creamy. Salt and pepper to taste. Finish with butter and grated Parmigiano-Reggiano.

risotto primavera [ree-SOH-toh pree-mah-VAIR-uh]
Italian origin. Sauté onions with saffron until translucent. Add
chicken stock, Arborio rice, and white wine. Stir slowly to cook and
release starch. Keep soft and creamy. Salt and pepper to taste. Finish
with butter and grated Parmigiano-Reggiano. Slowly mix in sautéed
spring or summer vegetables such as zucchini, peas, artichokes,
asparagus, or French green beans.

robe de chambre [rohb duh SHAHM-bruh]
French origin. Wash potato and poke a hole in it. Steam whole.

roschti [ROOSH-tee] (see rösti)

rösti [ROO-stee]
Swiss origin. Similar to potato pancakes. Prepare a mixture of grated
potatoes. Salt and pepper to taste. (If desired, add bacon, onions,
cheese, or herbs.) Sauté and finish in oven.

scalloped potatoes (see potatoes au gratin)

shoestring potatoes (see pommes paille)

soubise [soo-BEEZ]
French origin. Sauté chopped onions until translucent. Add béchamel.
Simmer 30 minutes. Process with hand blender. Salt and pepper to taste.

spaetzle; spatzle [SHPETS-luh]
Eastern European origin. Make a slightly liquid batter with 8 oz flour,
2 eggs, salt and pepper, and water. Pour batter through colander into
boiling salted water. Shock in ice water. Sauté.

spanakopita [span-uh-KOH-pih-tuh]
Greek origin. Mix feta and Kefalotiri (or other Greek cheese) with eggs,
dill, salt, and pepper. Wrap in triangles of phyllo dough or make a pie.

Spanish rice
American origin. Sauté bacon, onions, bell peppers, and garlic. Add
1 volume of uncooked rice. Toss in fat until translucent. Add 2 cups
of water or stock, tomatoes, paprika, salt, and pepper. Bring to a boil.
Cover and transfer to oven. Bake 20 minutes. Fluff rice.

succotash [SUHK-uh-tash]
Native American origin. Many regional variations. Sauté onions,
tomatoes, and red and green peppers. Add parboiled lima beans and
corn. (If desired, add other beans.) Serve hot or cold.

Sides

sushi rice
Japanese origin. Wash 2 cups of short-grain rice 3 times. Add an equal amount of water. Bring to boil, then simmer 15 minutes. Let rest 10 minutes. Heat 2 tablespoons rice vinegar with 2 tablespoons sugar. Add the vinegar-sugar mixture to the rice. Cool.

sweet potato casserole
American origin (Southern). Many variations. Sauté onions. Add diced sweet potatoes and water or stock. Cover and simmer. Mash sweet potatoes. Put in ovenproof dish. Top with pecans, butter, and brown sugar. Bake au gratin.

Tex-Mex potatoes
Bake potatoes. Top with Monterey jack, ground cumin, and cilantro.

timbale [TIM-bahl]
French origin. Blanch, boil, or sauté thinly diced vegetables. Place loosely into buttered ramekin. Make a custard using 3 eggs per cup of cream. Salt and pepper to taste. Pour custard over vegetables. Bake in bain-marie at 325°F until set. Serve warm.

tomate farcie [toh-MAHT fahr-SEE]
Stuffed tomato.

tomates Provençales [toh-MAHT proh-vahn-SAHL]
French origin (Provence). Halve tomatoes. Sprinkle tops with chopped garlic, breadcrumbs, chopped parsley, salt, and pepper. Drizzle with olive oil. Bake at 350°F.

tomato concassée [kon-kah-SAY]
French origin. Sauté diced onions. Add skinless, seedless diced tomatoes. Add garlic, bay leaf, and sugar for acidity correction. Salt and pepper to taste. Reduce until slightly dry.

tomatoes Provençal [proh-vahn-SAHL] (see tomates Provençales)

tostones [tohs-TOHN-ehs]
Caribbean/Latin American origin. Slice plantains on the bias. Deep-fry to blanch. Pat-dry. Pound out. Deep-fry again. Serve warm.

truffade [troo-FAHD]
French origin (Auvergne). Blanch potatoes. Slice. Sauté in garlic. (If desired, add bacon.) Shallow-fry sliced potatoes. Mix in Cantal or similar cheese and make a crust. Serve warm.

Sides

Tuscan beans

Rinse and soak dried cannellini or other Italian beans. Add water, sage, garlic, and extra-virgin olive oil. Simmer until beans are tender. Salt and pepper to taste.

vegetable curry

Indian origin. Many variations. Pan-fry curry spices such as turmeric, red chili powder, coriander, cumin, fenugreek, pepper, allspice, nutmeg, mace, and cardamom in ghee or oil. Add vegetables such as carrots, cauliflower, broccoli, red peppers, potatoes, and turnips. Sauté grated onions. Deglaze with water. Add tomatoes. Simmer until vegetables are tender. Finish with coconut milk.

Venetian rice (see risi e bisi)

yellow rice

Sauté turmeric, cumin, and saffron. Add rice and water. Simmer. Salt and pepper to taste.

The Chef's Répertoire Desserts

à la mode [ah lah MOHD]
> In the fashion of. American origin. Add scoop of ice cream on a piece of pie and serve.

amaretti [am-ah-RET-tee]
> Italian origin. Similar to macaroon. Beat 1 egg white with 4 oz almond paste and ½ cup sugar until smooth. Pipe cookies on silicone mat. Bake at 375°F until risen and golden in color with tiny cracks. Cool on rack. Serve at room temperature or freeze for later use.

angel cake (see angel food cake)

angel food cake
> Make a meringue with 12 egg whites and 1¾ cups sugar. Fold in 1 cup sifted cake flour. (If desired, add flavorings or extracts.) Bake in tube pan at 350°F until golden and cooked through. Cool on rack. Serve warm, at room temperature, or freeze for later use.

apple strudel [STROO-duhl]
> German origin. Quick-sauté quartered apples and mix with ¾ cup bread crumbs, 1 cup sugar, ½ cup walnuts, ⅓ cup currants, and cinnamon to taste. Roll mixture into a rectangle of layered phyllo dough. Brush with melted butter. Bake at 400°F until golden brown.

baba au rhum [bah-bah oh RUHM]
> French origin. Dissolve ¼ oz fresh yeast in ⅓ cup milk. Heat. Mix 1¾ cups flour, 3 eggs, 1 teaspoon sugar, and milk/yeast mix. Knead. Add 5 tablespoons fresh butter. Allow to rise. Place in individual baba molds. Allow to rise again. Glaze with egg yolks. Bake at 350°F until golden. Unmold. Saturate with rum syrup. Serve at room temperature.

baked Alaska
> Soften ice cream to shape it into a cake pan. Top with sponge cake and freeze. Unmold and plate with sponge cake at the bottom. Pipe soft meringue to cover entirety of ice cream and sponge cake. Flambé and serve immediately.

baklava [bahk-lah-VAH]
> Greek/Middle Eastern origin. Process nuts into coarse consistency. Layer sheets of phyllo dough with butter. Sprinkle chopped nuts onto every eighth layer and finish layering. Precut into diamond shapes. Bake at 350°F for 50 minutes. When golden, pour sauce on top. To make sauce, boil 1 cup sugar with 1 cup water, ½ cup honey, and vanilla to taste.

Desserts

bananas Foster
American origin (New Orleans). Add butter and brown sugar to sauté pan and cook. Add cinnamon and nutmeg. Add lengthwise-sliced ripe bananas and cook. Flambé with liquor. Serve with vanilla ice cream. (If desired, add whipped cream.)

banana split
Cut banana lengthwise. Top banana with vanilla, chocolate, and strawberry ice cream. Top with syrups. Garnish with nuts, whipped cream, and maraschino cherries.

banoffee pie; banoffi pie; banoffy pie
English origin. Prepare dulce de leche (unopened cans of condensed milk boiled in water for 3½ hours) ahead of time. Make pastry dough with 9 oz flour, 1 oz icing sugar, 4½ oz butter, and 1 egg yolk. Bake à blanc. To assemble, spread dulce de leche over pastry base. Arrange banana slices over the dulce de leche. Top bananas with whipped cream mixed with instant coffee and sugar.

Bavarian cream
Soften 2 tablespoons gelatin in ½ cup water. Whisk 4 egg yolks with ½ cup sugar. Add 2 cups of hot milk. Add gelatin. Cool. Add 2 cups of heavy cream, whipped. Chill.

bavarois [bah-vahr-WAH] (see Bavarian cream)

beignets [ben-YAY]
1. French origin. Heat 1 cup water with ½ cup butter. Add 1 cup flour, 1 tablespoon sugar, and salt to taste. Stir. Add 5 eggs, integrating one at a time. Deep-fry. Drain. Cool. Dust with powdered sugar.
2. American origin (New Orleans). Mix 1 envelope active dry yeast, ¾ cup water, and ¼ cup granulated sugar in food processor. Add 1 egg, ½ cup evaporated milk, and salt to taste. Mix. Add 3½ cups flour and ⅛ cup shortening until dough consistency. Reserve and let rise overnight. Roll out rectangles. Let rise for 1 hour. Fry until golden.

biscotti [bee-SKOH-tee]
Italian origin. Combine 2 cups flour, ½ cup sugar, ½ teaspoon baking powder, ½ teaspoon baking soda, 3 eggs, and salt to taste. Add flavorings or extracts. (If desired, add almonds, pistachios, or raisins.) Knead. Roll on silicone mat and brush with egg whites. Bake at 350°F until golden. Let cool on rack. Slice and toast. Serve at room temperature.

Desserts

biscuit dough
American origin. Mix 1⅓ cups flour, 2 tablespoons sugar, 1½ teaspoons baking powder, and salt to taste. Add 5 tablespoons butter and ⅔ cup heavy cream. Knead.

black forest cake
German origin. Beat ½ cup butter and 1½ cups sugar. Add 2 eggs. Add 1⅔ cups flour, ⅔ cup cocoa powder, 1½ teaspoons baking soda, and 1½ cups buttermilk. Bake in round cake pans at 350°F until golden and cooked through. Cool on rack. Spray each layer with liquor. To assemble, add whipped cream and cherries to each layer. Decorate with chocolate shavings.

blancmange [bluh-MAHNZH] (see blanc-manger)

blanc-manger [bluh-MAHN-zhay]
Many variations. Heat 4 cups cream or milk with ½ cup sugar. Infuse with almond extract. Add two packets of gelatin. Pour in cups or ramekins. Chill.

bombe; bombe glacée [BAWMB glah-say]
French origin. Soften one or more kinds of ice cream. Press in a bowl. (If desired, create a sponge cake bottom.) Freeze. Serve cold.

bombe [BAWMB] **Alaska** (see baked Alaska)

Boston cream pie
American origin (Northeastern). Make a sponge cake. Separate in two. Top one layer with thick pastry cream. Place other layer on top. Pour hot ganache over the top. Chill.

bouchée [boo-SHAY]
French origin. Make two rounds from a puff pastry sheet. Cut a smaller round inside one of the rounds and remove excess. Brush both rounds with egg yolks. Stack the smaller round on top of the larger round. Transfer to silicone mat. Bake until golden and dry on the outside and moist on the inside. Fill with pastry cream and fresh fruits.

bread and butter pudding
British origin. Butter bread slices and layer in ovenproof dish. Pour batter of 4 cups milk, 6 eggs, and ½ cup sugar over bread. Bake at 350°F until golden and cooked through. Serve warm or cold.

brioche [BREE-ohsh]

French origin. Combine 1½ cups flour, 1¼ cups bread flour, 1 teaspoon salt, and 2 tablespoons sugar. Dissolve 1 oz fresh yeast in warm water. Add dissolved yeast to flour mixture. Add 4 eggs and mix well. Add 8 oz butter and knead thoroughly. Let dough rise and double in size. Refrigerate overnight. Give dough two turns, then shape into one large ball and one smaller ball. Place larger ball in a prepared brioche mold. Place the smaller ball on top. Glaze with egg wash. Bake at 425°F. Cool on rack.

brown betty

American origin. Mix bread crumbs with melted butter, brown sugar, and cinnamon. (If desired, add additional spices.) Layer apples or other fruits with bread crumb mixture. Cover and bake at 350°F for 1 hour. (If desired, add a custard to the layering.)

brownie

American origin. Mix ¾ cup butter, 1½ cups sugar, 3 eggs, ⅓ cup cocoa powder, ¾ cup flour, ½ teaspoon baking powder, salt, and 1 cup chocolate chips. (If desired, add toasted nuts.) Bake in sheet pan at 350°F. Cool. Serve at room temperature.

bûche de Noël [BOOSH duh noh-EL] (see yule log)

buckle

American origin. For the topping, process ½ cup sugar, 6 tablespoons flour, 4 tablespoons butter, nutmeg, and salt. For batter A, whisk together 1¾ cups flour, 2 teaspoons baking powder, and salt. For batter B, whisk together 4 tablespoons butter, 1 cup sugar, 1 egg, ½ cup milk, and vanilla. Add batter A to batter B. Fold in fruits such as peaches, pears, or cherries. Pour into buttered oven dish. Add topping. Bake at 350°F for 45 minutes.

butter cake

Similar to chiffon cake. Beat 2¼ cups sifted cake flour, 1½ cups sugar, 1 tablespoon baking powder, and salt to taste. Beat in 6 egg yolks and ¾ cup clarified butter. (If desired, add flavorings and extracts.) Fold in 6 whipped egg whites. Bake in tube pan at 325°F until golden and cooked through. Cool on rack. Serve warm, at room temperature, or freeze for later use.

Desserts

buttercream frosting
  1. American version. Whip 1 cup butter. Add ½ cup confectioner·
  sugar and mix. (If desired, add food coloring and flavorings.) Use at
  room temperature or chill and reserve for later use.
  2. European version. Make an Italian meringue with 2 cups sugar,
  ½ cup water, and 8 egg whites. When meringue is cooling down,
  add 4 cups diced fresh butter. (If desired, blend in extracts or
  flavorings.)

canelé [kan-eh-LAY]
  French origin (Bordeaux). Make a custard with 3 eggs, 1 cup sugar,
  ¾ cup flour, vanilla, rum, and 2 cups hot milk. Pour in canelé molds or
  ramekins. Bake in bain-marie at 250°F until slightly brown. Unmold.

cannoli [kan-OH-lee]
  Italian origin (Sicily). Make dough by mixing 1 cup flour,
  3 tablespoons sugar, 1 teaspoon cocoa powder, cinnamon, ⅛ teaspoon
  baking soda, 1 lb butter, and 1 egg. Pass through pasta maker to
  obtain thin, oval-shaped dough. Roll around a tube. Deep-fry. Cool.
  Fill with ricotta, goat cheese, sugar, and orange-peel filling.

caramel
  Cook sugar with just enough water to wet. When light brown, take off heat.

caramel sauce
  Mix 1 cup sugar and ½ cup water. Pour in 2 cups cream. Heat to
  homogeneous mix. Serve warm or chilled.

carrot cake
  Beat 4 eggs, one at a time, into 1½ cups sugar. Add 1 cup oil. Then
  add 2 cups flour, 1 teaspoon baking soda, 1½ teaspoons baking
  powder, and salt and cinnamon to taste. Fold in ¾ lb grated carrots
  and 1 cup chopped pecans. Bake at 350°F until golden and cooked
  through. Cool on rack. Serve warm, at room temperature, or freeze
  for later use. (If desired, frost cake.)

charlotte [SHAHR-luht]
  British origin. Soak ladyfingers in syrup and then layer in soufflé dish
  with softened ice cream and fruit mousse (¾ cup fruit purée, 1 cup
  cream, and ¼ oz gelatin). Top with sponge cake and press. Chill.
  Unmold before serving. Serve cold.

charlotte russe [SHAHR-luht ROOS] (see charlotte)

chausson aux pommes [shoh-SAHN oh PUM] (see turnover)

cheesecake
   1. Cooked version. Many variations. Beat 8 oz cream cheese with
   1½ cups sugar. Add 1 cup milk and 4 eggs. Add ¼ cup flour and
   flavorings or extracts. Line cake pan with graham cracker crust. Pour
   in filling. Bake in bain-marie at 350°F.
   2. Uncooked version. Many variations. Beat 8 oz cream cheese with
   1 cup sugar. Add 1 cup sweetened condensed milk. Dissolve
   1 package of gelatin in 1 cup boiling water. Add gelatin mixture to
   cream cheese mixture. Add flavorings or extracts. Line cake pan with
   graham cracker crust. Pour in filling. Chill.

cherries jubilee
   French origin. Sauté Bing cherries in butter and sugar. Flambé with
   Kirsch. Deglaze with water. Thicken with cornstarch. Serve with
   vanilla ice cream.

chiffon cake
   Similar to butter cake. Beat 2¼ cups sifted cake flour, 1½ cups sugar,
   1 tablespoon baking powder, and salt to taste. Beat 6 egg yolks in ½ cup
   vegetable oil. (If desired, add flavorings and extracts.) Fold in 6 whipped
   egg whites. Bake in tube pan at 325°F until golden and cooked through. Cool
   on rack. Serve warm, at room temperature, or freeze for later use.

chocolate croissant (see pain au chocolat)

chocolate mousse
   Add 2 egg yolks to 5 oz ganache. Make a meringue with 2 egg whites and
   3 tablespoons sugar. Fold in ganache. Fold in ½ cup cream, whipped. Chill.

choux à la crème [SHOO ah lah KREM] (see cream puffs)

choux [SHOO] **pastry**
   Heat ½ cup water, ½ cup milk, 4 oz butter, and salt. Add 1 cup flour
   and stir. Keep cooking the dough to eliminate moisture. Cool. Add
   4 eggs, integrating one at a time.

churro [CHOO-roh]
   Spanish origin. Heat 1 cup water, ½ cup butter, and salt. Add
   1 cup flour and stir. Add 3 eggs. Pipe into deep-fryer. Drain on paper
   towels. Roll in sugar. Serve immediately.

Desserts

clafouti [kla-foo-TEE]

French origin. Mix 4 eggs, ¾ cup flour, ¾ cup sugar, 1 cup milk, rum, and vanilla. Place cherries or other fruits into a buttered oven dish. Pour batter over fruit. Bake at 350°F for 45 minutes.

cobbler

American origin. Cook fruits with sugar, cornstarch, cinnamon, and other spices. Cover with biscuit dough. Bake at 375°F for 45 minutes. Serve with whipped cream or vanilla ice cream.

cobbler dough (see biscuit dough)

cream pie

Line pie pan with flaky pastry. Make pudding by mixing ⅔ cup sugar, ¼ cup cornstarch, salt, 2½ cup milk, and 5 egg yolks. Simmer until thick. Add flavorings or extracts. (If desired, add fruit.) Pour pudding into pastry crust. (If desired, top with meringue.) Bake at 325°F for 10 minutes. Cool. Serve chilled.

cream puffs

Pipe round dollops of choux pastry on silicone mat. Bake at 400°F until puffed up, dried, and golden. Cool. Pipe in pastry cream or whipped cream to fill puffs. (If desired, dip halfway in caramel or fondant to decorate.) Serve cold.

crema catalana [KRAY-ma ka-tah-LAN-uh] (see crème catalane)

crema pasticciera [KREM-a pa-stit-SEE-air-uh] (see pastry cream)

crème anglaise [KREM ahn-GLEZ]

French origin. Mix 3 egg yolks with ¼ cup sugar. Add 1¼ cup hot milk and vanilla. Cook at temperature below egg coagulation until nappéd. Add liqueur. Chill.

crème bavaroise [KREM bah-vahr-WAHZ] (see Bavarian cream)

crème brûlée [KREM broo-LAY]

French origin. Whisk 4 egg yolks with ½ cup sugar. Add flavorings or extracts. Add 2 cups boiling hot cream. Bake in ramekins in bain-marie until set. Chill. Dust with sugar. Caramelize with butane torch. Serve immediately.

crème caramel [KREM ka-RUH-mel] (see flan)

Desserts

crème catalane [KREM ka-TAH-lan]
Spanish origin (Catalonia). Similar to crème brulée. Slowly heat
milk, cinnamon stick, lemon or orange zest, and vanilla until mixture
begins to thicken. Do not boil. Pour into shallow ovenproof dishes
and allow to cool. Refrigerate for several hours. Immediately before
serving, scatter sugar evenly over each serving. Caramelize under a
broiler or with a butane torch and serve.

crème pâtissière [KREM pah-tee-SYAIR] (see pastry cream)

crêpes [KREP]
French origin. Make a batter with 1 cup flour, 2 eggs, ½ cup milk,
½ cup water, 2 tablespoons melted butter, rum, salt, and orange zest.
Sauté thin crêpes. Serve immediately.

crêpes Suzette [KREP soo-ZET]
Sauté crêpes. Fold in the pan. Add butter and sugar. Deglaze with
orange juice. Flambé with Grand Marnier.

crisp
American origin. Proceed as with crumble but omit oatmeal.

croissant [KWAH-sahn]
Crescent. Dissolve 2½ teaspoons active dry yeast with 1 cup warm
milk and 1 tablespoon sugar. Reserve. Make a well in 2¼ cups flour,
salt, and 2 tablespoons fresh butter. Pour the milk/yeast mix into
the well. Make a dough and knead. Roll dough into a ¾-inch thick
rectangle. Place 12 oz butter on one long side of the rectangle. Fold
dough over to completely secure butter inside. Roll out into a thinner
rectangle. Make two folds. Then fold the three sections onto each
other. Make another three turns, resting the dough in between turns.
To cut and shape, roll out the dough and cut into triangles. Roll
triangles onto themselves, starting with the base. Shape into crescents.
Place on silicone mat. Let rise at room temperature until volume
increases 50%. Brush with egg wash. Bake at 375°F until golden.

croquembouche [kroh-kuhm-BOOSH]
French origin. Make cream puffs with choux pastry. Fill with pastry
cream. Superpose cream puffs into a high cone shape, binding puffs with
caramel. Decorate with caramel, sugared almonds, and marzipan ribbons.

crostata [kroh-STA-tah]

Italian origin. Roll out shortbread pastry dough into circle. Place on silicone mat. Spread jam on dough. Toss summer fruits such as plums or peaches with sugar and flour. Distribute fruit evenly over dough. Bake at 350°F until dough is golden brown. Serve warm, at room temperature, or chilled.

crumble

British origin. Simmer a fruit combination such as apples, peaches, rhubarb, and plums. Sweeten with sugar and thicken with cornstarch. (If desired, add dry fruits such as raisins.) Transfer to ovenproof dish. Make a topping by combining ¾ cup flour, ¾ cup brown sugar, cinnamon, salt, ¾ cup rolled oats, ⅓ cup chopped nuts, and ½ cup butter. Spread topping onto fruit mixture. Bake at 375°F until golden brown and crisp. Serve warm or at room temperature with whipped cream or vanilla ice cream.

crumpet

British origin. Dissolve 2 teaspoons dry active yeast in warm water. Make a dough with 3 cups flour, 2 tablespoons powdered milk, salt, and the yeast mixture. Allow to rise and bubble. Mix 1 teaspoon baking soda and 2 tablespoons water. Add to dough and allow to rise again. Sauté in metal rings until dough appears dry on both sides. Cool on rack.

crumple (see buckle)

crunch (see crisp)

cupcake

American origin. Beat ½ cup butter with ⅔ cup sugar. Add 3 eggs. Then add 1½ cups flour and 1½ teaspoons baking powder. Fill muffin cups. Bake at 350°F until golden brown. Cool on rack. To serve, pipe buttercream frosting on top.

custard pie

American origin. Line a pie pan with flaky pastry. Make a custard with 3 eggs, 2 egg yolks, ½ cup sugar, vanilla, and 2 cups hot milk. Pour custard into pie crust. Bake at 325°F until custard is set.

dacquoise [da-KWAHZ]

Flavor meringue with almond extract. Pipe 2 or 3 large disks of meringue on silicone mat. Bake at 200°F until light and hard. Assemble disks with whipped cream or buttercream in between. Add fresh fruits like strawberries. Dust with confectioners' sugar.

dulce de leche [DOOL-chay day LE-chay]
Spanish origin. Boil cans of sweetened condensed milk in water for
4 hours. Cool. Open. Serve warm or chilled.

éclair [ay-KLAIR]
French origin. Pipe logs of choux pastry on silicone mat. Bake at
400°F until puffed up, dried, and golden. Cool. Pipe pastry cream or
whipped cream to fill. (If desired, dip halfway in caramel or fondant
to decorate.) Serve cold.

fairy cake (see cupcake)
British origin.

feuilletage [foo-yuh-TAHZH] (see puff pastry)

financier [fee-nahn-SYAY]
French origin. Mix ¼ cup flour, ½ cup ground almonds, ¾ cup
confectioners' sugar, ⅓ cup beurre noisette, salt, and 3 egg whites.
Bake in losange molds at 350°F until brown and cooked through.

flaky pastry
Make a dough with 2½ cups flour, 1 teaspoon sugar, 4 oz butter, salt
to taste, and enough cold water to bind.

flame on the iceberg
Similar to baked Alaska. Top sponge cake with vanilla ice cream. Top
with whipped cream. Flambé and serve immediately.

flan
French origin. Make flan mix with ½ cup sugar and 2 eggs per cup
of milk. Reserve. Make caramel and pour in the bottom of individual
ramekins. Then pour in the flan mix. Bake in bain-marie at 300°F
until set.

Florentine [FLOHR-uhn-teen] **cookies**
French origin. Mix 4 oz toasted and chopped hazelnuts, 4 oz
almonds, 4 oz candied fruits, ⅓ cup flour, and spices such as nutmeg
and cinnamon. Reserve. Cook ½ cup sugar with ½ cup honey. Mix
into nuts and fruits. Spread on silicone mat. Bake at 350°F until lacy
and golden. Cool. Half-dip each cookie in melted chocolate. Cool
and serve. Variation: Spread melted chocolate on one side of each
cookie or drizzle lines of melted chocolate across each cookie.

frangipane [FRAN-juh-pan] (see frangipani)

frangipani [fran-juh-PAN-ee]
Italian origin. Process ½ cup ground almonds, ¼ cup sugar, 1 egg, 3 tablespoons butter, and 1 tablespoon flour.

French toast
French origin. Make batter with 4 eggs, 1 cup milk, 1 teaspoon sugar, and a pinch of salt. Dip slice of bread in batter. Sauté on griddle until golden and cooked through. Serve with butter, maple syrup, and confectioners' sugar.

fried ice cream
Similar to baked Alaska. Hard freeze a scoop of ice cream. Dip in beaten eggs, then cookie crumbs or Japanese bread crumbs. Deep-fry and serve immediately.

frosting, cream cheese
Beat 8 oz cream cheese and ¼ cup butter. Add 2 cups sifted confectioners' sugar and whip.

fruit cake
English origin. Beat 1 cup butter and 1 cup brown sugar. Add 3 eggs. Add brandy, orange zest, 2 cups chopped nuts, 6 cups dried fruits, 2 cups flour, and 1 teaspoon baking powder. Bake at 325°F until golden and cooked through. Cool on rack. Serve warm, at room temperature, or freeze for later use.

galette [gah-LET]
Roll shortbread pastry dough into extra-wide circle. Place on silicone mat. Toss summer fruits such as plums or peaches with sugar and flour. Distribute fruits evenly over the dough. Fold dough edges over fruits in a rustic way. Bake at 350°F until dough is golden brown. Cool. Serve warm, at room temperature, or chilled.

ganache [gah-NAHSH]
French origin. Bring 1 cup cream to a boil. Take off the heat. Add 1 cup chocolate pellets. Rest. Process with hand blender until smooth. (If desired, add flavoring with liquor.) Chill.

genoise [zhen-WAHZ]
Italian origin. Similar to sponge cake. Beat 4 eggs and ½ cup sugar over water bath until a thick ribbon forms. Flavor with liquor or extract. Fold in 1 cup sifted flour. Then fold in ¼ cup clarified butter. Bake in cake pan at 350°F until golden and cooked through. Cool on rack. Serve warm, at room temperature, or freeze for later use.

gingerbread
Mix 2⅓ cups flour, ⅓ cup sugar, 1 cup molasses, ¾ cup hot water, ½ cup butter, 1 egg, 1 teaspoon baking soda, salt, ginger, and cinnamon. Bake at 325°F until golden and cooked through.

graham cracker crust
Mix 1¼ cup graham crackers, 2 tablespoons sugar, and 5 tablespoons melted butter. Press into pie pan. Chill for later use or bake at 350°F.

granité [grah-nee-TAY]
Process 16 fl oz fruit juice, 6 oz fruit pulp, and ¼ cup liquor such as Grand Marnier or rum. Freeze overnight. Scrape with fork and serve immediately.

grunt
American origin. Mix berries or other fruits with sugar. Pour into a soufflé dish and top with a layer of grunt dough. Cover and place the soufflé dish in a pot big enough to contain the entire dish. Add water to the pot and steam the grunt for 1½ hours. Unmold and serve warm.

grunt dough
American origin. Mix together 1¼ cups flour, 2 tablespoons sugar, 1¼ teaspoons baking powder, ½ teaspoon salt, 3 tablespoons butter, and ½ cup milk. Knead.

ice cream pie
American origin. Line pie pan with graham cracker crust and bake. Cool and chill. Soften ice cream. Pack into pie crust. Top with whipped cream. Serve immediately.

île flottante [eel floh-TAHN]
Floating island. French origin. Make a meringue. Poach in vanilla-infused milk. To serve, add meringue on top of crème anglaise. (If desired, add toasted almonds or spun sugar.)

key lime pie

American origin (Florida). Line a pie pan with graham cracker crust or pâte sablée. To make filling, beat 3 egg yolks. Add 14 oz sweetened condensed milk, key lime zest, and ½ cup key lime juice to the eggs. Add filling to pie crust. Bake at 350°F until set. Cool. Top with piped meringue.

küchen [KOO-kun]

German-American origin. Whisk 8 tablespoons butter into ¾ cup sugar. Add 2 eggs. Add 1 cup flour, 1 tablespoon baking powder, and salt. Pour batter into oven dish. Top with summer fruits, sugar, and pecans. Bake at 350°F for 45 minutes.

kugel [KOO-guhl]

Jewish origin. Both sweet and savory variations. Make a pudding of potatoes or egg noodles, chopped vegetables or fruits, cottage or cream cheese, and a savory or sweet egg batter. Bake au gratin.

ladyfingers

Make a sponge cake batter and increase the amount of flour by 10%. Pipe into finger-shaped cookies on silicone mat and dust with sugar. Bake at 350°F until firm and barely brown. Cool on rack. Serve at room temperature.

langue de chat [lahng duh SHAH] (see ladyfingers)

linzer tart

Austrian origin. Make a flaky pastry dough with 1 cup ground almonds, 1 cup ground hazelnuts, 1½ cup flour, ⅔ cup sugar, ½ teaspoon baking powder, and 7 oz butter. Line pie pan with rolled-out dough. Fill with homemade raspberry preserves. Top with lattice crust. Bake at 350°F until dough is golden brown. Cool. Serve warm, at room temperature, or chilled.

macaron [ma-kuh-ROHN]

French origin. Similar to amaretti. Mix 8 oz icing sugar and 4.5 oz sifted almond flour. Make a meringue with 4 egg whites and 1 oz granulated sugar. (If desired, add food coloring.) Fold meringue into flour mix. Pipe cookies on silicone mat. Bake at 300°F until light brown. Cool. Peel off. Pipe buttercream onto flat side of macaron and top with another macaron to make a sandwich. Serve at room temperature.

macaroon (see macaron)

macaroon, coconut
American origin. Beat 4 egg whites, 1 cup sugar, and salt to taste in double boiler. Off heat, add flavorings and extracts, ½ cup sifted cake flour, and 2 cups sweetened coconut. Form cookies on silicone mat. Bake at 325°F until golden brown.

madeleine [mad-LEN]
French origin. Beat 3 eggs and ⅔ cup sugar into a thick ribbon and flavor with orange flower. Fold in 1 cup sifted flour. Fold in ½ cup clarified butter. Bake in Madeleine pan at 350°F until golden and cooked through. Cool on rack. Serve warm, at room temperature, or freeze for later use.

maracoon (see macaron)

meringue, French style
Use 4 tablespoons sugar per egg white. Beat into stiff peaks. Use as is (soft meringue) or pipe on silicone mat and bake at 200°F until light and hard (hard meringue). Variation: Poach instead of baking.

meringue, hard (see meringue, Swiss, Italian, and French styles)

meringue, Italian style
Use 2 tablespoons sugar per egg white. Cook sugar until 240°F. Add syrup while beating egg whites into stiff peaks. Keep beating until room temperature. Use as is (soft meringue) or pipe on silicone mat and bake at 200°F until light and hard (hard meringue). Variation: Poach instead of baking.

meringue, soft (see meringue, Swiss, Italian, and French styles)

meringue, Swiss style
Use ¼ cup sugar per egg white. Mix sugar and egg whites. Whisk into stiff peaks over double boiler at 130°F. Transfer to mixer and beat until room temperature. Use as is (soft meringue) or pipe on silicone mat and bake at 200°F until light and hard (hard meringue). Variation: Poach instead of baking.

mille-feuille [meel-FOY]
French origin. Roll out puff pastry. Place on silicone mat. Poke holes in pastry with fork. Bake at 400°F until puffed, dried, and light golden. Cool. Cut three 16 × 12-inch rectangles. Spread thick pastry cream on one rectangle. Top with the second rectangle. Spread thick pastry cream on top of the second rectangle. Top with the third rectangle, flat side up. Chill. To serve, slice the edges off and dust with powdered sugar. (If desired, top with fondant and warm chocolate ganache.)

mince pie
Simmer apples, raisins, pecans, sugar, cider, brandy, cinnamon, nutmeg, and butter until dry and glazed. Line pie crust with flaky pastry. Pour the glazed fruits on the pastry. Cover with second pastry crust. Egg wash. Bake at 350°F until golden brown. Serve warm.

molten chocolate
Beat 3 egg yolks and ⅓ cup sugar. Fold in 6 oz melted chocolate. Then fold in 3 egg whites. Bake at 400°F in individual ramekins. Serve immediately.

mousse au chocolat [oh shawk-aw-LAH] (see chocolate mousse)

muffin
Many variations. Whisk 1 cup sugar, ½ cup oil, 1 egg, and 1 cup yogurt. Add 12½ oz cake flour, 1 teaspoon baking soda, 2 teaspoons baking powder, and salt. Add fresh fruits such as blueberries or bananas. Bake in muffin tins at 400°F until golden and cooked through. Cool on racks.

Napoléon [na-poh-LAY-uhn] (see mille-feuille)

Norwegian omelet (see baked Alaska)

nougat [NOO-guht] (see turrón)

oeufs à la neige [UWF ah lah nezh] (see île flottante)

omelette Norvégienne [nohr-vay-JYEN] (see baked Alaska)

pain au chocolat [PEHN oh shawk-aw-LAH]
French origin. Dissolve 2½ teaspoons active dry yeast with 1 cup warm milk and 1 tablespoon sugar. Make a well in 2¼ cups flour, salt, and 2 tablespoons fresh butter. Pour the milk/yeast mix into the well. Make a dough and knead. Roll out dough into a ¾-inch thick rectangle. Place 12 oz of rectangular-shaped butter onto one long side of the rectangle. Fold over to completely secure butter inside the dough. Roll out into a thinner rectangle. Make two folds and then fold the three sections onto each other. (This counts as one turn.) Make another three turns, resting the dough in between turns. To cut and shape, roll out the dough and cut into 4-inch squares. Arrange chocolate bar on top of each square and roll into a cylinder. Transfer to silicone mat and let rise at room temperature until volume increases 50%. Brush with egg wash. Bake at 375°F until golden. Serve at room temperature or slightly warm.

Desserts

pain perdu [pehn pair-DOO] (see French toast)

pan di spagna [PAN dee SPAN-yuh] (see sponge cake)

pancakes
Make a batter with 2 cups flour, 2½ teaspoons baking powder, 3 tablespoons sugar, salt, 2 eggs, 1½ cups milk, and 2 tablespoons butter. Cook on griddle. Serve hot with maple syrup.

pandowdy
American origin. Cook fruits with sugar, cornstarch, cinnamon, and other spices. Cover with flaky pastry. Bake at 350°F for 1 hour. Serve with whipped cream or vanilla ice cream.

panettone [pan-eh-TOH-neh]
Italian origin. Make a dough with 1 oz baker's yeast, 3 oz flour, and enough water to bind. Let rise. Add 1 cup flour, ½ cup warm water, and knead. Let rise. Reserve. Make a sabayon in a double boiler with 7 tablespoons sugar, 1 egg, and 5 egg yolks. Add 1 cup flour and knead. Assemble two doughs. Add raisins. Place in a mold and let rise. Bake at 400°F until cooked through and golden.

panna cotta [PAN-nah KOH-tah]
Italian origin. Heat 4 cups cream with ½ cup sugar. Infuse with vanilla beans. Dissolve two packets of gelatin in cold water. Add to cream and sugar mixture. Pour in cups or ramekins. Chill.

panqué [pan-KAY] (see pound cake)

parfait [pahr-FAY]
Marinate fresh fruits such as berries or bananas. Layer in dessert glass with whipped cream, yogurt, mascarpone, or any combination of these.

Paris-Brest [pa-ree BREST]
French origin. Pipe a 3-inch wide, 8- to 10-inch circle of choux pastry on silicone mat and top with toasted flaked almonds. Bake at 400°F until golden and puffed up. Once cooked, slice in half horizontally. Cover bottom pastry shell with pastry cream, then whipped cream. (If desired, use coffee- or praline-flavored buttercream.) Cover with top pastry shell and dust with confectioners' sugar.

Desserts

pastry cream
French origin. Mix 3 egg yolks with ¼ cup sugar. Add ⅛ cup flour. Then add 1¼ cup hot milk and vanilla. Cook at temperature below egg coagulation. Add liqueur. Chill.

pâte brisée [paht bree-ZAY] (see flaky pastry)

pâte feuilletée [paht foy-uh-TAY] (see puff pastry)

pâte sablée [paht sah-BLAY] (see shortbread pastry)

pâte sucrée [paht soo-KRAY] (see sweet flaky pastry)

Pavlova [pahv-LOH-vuh]
New Zealand origin. Pipe a large disk of meringue on silicone mat. Bake at 200°F until light and hard. Cool. Top with whipped cream and fresh fruit such as kiwis and strawberries.

peach Louis (see pêches Louis)

peach melba (see pêches melba)

pecan pie
American origin (Southern). Line a pie pan with flaky pastry. Mix 3 eggs, 1 cup sugar, 1 cup corn syrup, ¼ cup clarified butter, and salt. (If desired, add bourbon.) Add 2 cups toasted pecans. Pour mix into pie crust. Bake at 325°F until set.

pêches Louis [pesh LOO-ee]
French origin. Sauté peaches in butter and sugar. Flambé with cognac. Deglaze with water. Add cornstarch. Simmer and thicken. Serve with vanilla ice cream.

pêches melba [pesh MEL-bah]
French origin. Vanilla ice cream, poached peaches, and raspberry purée. (If desired, add spun sugar and toasted almonds.)

pièce montée [pee-es MAHN-tay] (see croquembouche)

pithivier [pee-tee-VYAY]
French origin. Make an 8- to 10-inch circle with uncooked puff pastry. Pipe frangipane onto the first circle, leaving a 1-inch gap on the outer edge. (If desired, hide a dry fava bean in the frangipane.) Top with second circle of puff pastry. Brush with egg wash. Make a chimney. Bake at 375°F until golden. Serve slightly warm or at room temperature.

Desserts

poire belle Hélène [pwahr BEL ay-LEN]
French origin. Poach pears. Make a ganache. To assemble, serve a
poached pear with a scoop of vanilla ice cream and a tuile cookie.
Pour warm ganache over the pear. Serve immediately.

popover
Make a batter with 1 tablespoon butter, 4¾ oz flour, salt, 2 eggs, and
1 cup milk. Bake in popover tins at 400°F until puffed up, dried, and
golden brown. Serve immediately.

porridge
Simmer oats until soft and creamy. Serve with milk, honey, sugar, and
fruits or syrup.

pot-au-crème [poht-oh-KREM]
French origin. Mix 2 eggs plus 1 yolk with ⅓ cup sugar. Slowly add
2 cups hot milk. Fill ramekins. Bake in bain-marie at 300°F until set.

pot de crème [poh duh KREM] (see pot-au-crème)

pound cake
Beat 1 cup butter with 1 cup sugar until fluffy. Add 4 eggs. Then add
1 cup cake flour, salt, and 2 teaspoons baking powder. Bake at 350°F
until golden and cooked through. Cool on rack. Serve warm, at room
temperature, or freeze for later use.

pound cake, British style (see pound cake)
British origin. Proceed as with pound cake and add dried fruits.

profiterole [proh-FEE-tuh-rohl]
French origin. Pipe round dollops of choux pastry on silicone mat.
Bake at 400°F until puffed up, dried, and golden. Cool. Slice in half.
Fill with vanilla ice cream. Plate. Sauce with chocolate sauce. Top
with toasted almonds. Serve immediately.

puff pastry
French origin. Make a dough with 8 oz of flour, salt, and cold water.
Weigh and reserve half. Roll out dough into a ¾-inch thick rectangle.
Place 12 oz of rectangular-shaped butter onto the one long side of
the rectangle. Fold over to completely secure butter inside the dough.
Roll out into a thinner rectangle. Make two folds and then fold the
three sections onto each other. (This counts as one turn.) Make
another six turns, resting the dough in the refrigerator between turns.
Reserve for later use.

pumpkin pie
American origin (Southern). Line a pie pan with flaky pastry. Make custard with 3 eggs, 2 cups pumpkin purée, 1½ cups cream, ½ cup sugar, ⅓ cup brown sugar, cinnamon, nutmeg, allspice, and salt. Pour custard onto pie crust. Bake at 325°F until custard is set.

quatre-quart [KAH-truh KAHR] (see pound cake)

queen of sheba
Beat butter and ⅔ cup sugar. Add 3 egg yolks. Add 4 oz melted chocolate and rum. Then add ⅔ cup ground almonds and ½ cup cake flour. Fold in whipped egg whites. Melt 4 oz chocolate with rum. Bake in round cake pan at 350°F until golden and cooked through. Cool on rack.

red velvet cake
American origin (Southern). Mix 2½ cups flour, 1½ cups sugar, 1 teaspoon baking soda, salt, and 1 teaspoon cocoa powder. Mix in 1½ cups vegetable oil, 1 cup buttermilk, 2 eggs, and red food coloring. Bake in round cake pans at 350°F until golden and cooked through. Cool on rack. Serve warm, at room temperature, or freeze for later use.

reine de saba [ren duh SAH-bah] (see queen of sheba)

rice pudding
Soak short-grain rice in 3 cups of milk. Whisk in 2 egg yolks, salt, ⅓ cup sugar, and vanilla bean. Slowly cook until thick and creamy.

riz à l'impératrice [REEZ ah lem-PAIR-ah-trees]
French origin. Wash and parboil 1½ cups short-grain rice. Finish cooking in milk and reserve. Make a sabayon with 7 egg yolks and ¾ cup sugar. Add softened gelatin and dissolve. Then add to rice. Add diced candied fruits. Fold in whipped cream and pour into a decorative mold. Refrigerate overnight. Unmold and serve cold.

roulade [roo-LAHD]
Make a sponge cake mix and bake on sheet pan at 350°F until golden and cooked through. Roll up while still warm. Once cooled, fill with whipped cream, buttercream, jam, or ganache. Serve chilled or at room temperature.

royal icing
Equal part egg whites and confectioners' sugar.

rugelach [RUHG-uh-luhk]
Little twists. Jewish origin. Process 8 oz cream cheese and 8 oz butter. Add ¼ cup sugar, salt, and 2 cups flour. Rest the dough. Roll dough in small triangular shapes. Sprinkle with apricot preserves, brown sugar, cinnamon, raisins, and walnuts. Roll out like a croissant. Egg wash. Bake at 350°F.

sabayon [sah-bah-YAWN]
French origin. Beat 1 egg yolk, 2 tablespoons sugar, and 3 tablespoons sweet wine over a double boiler. Emulsify by whipping until homogeneous yet below temperature of egg coagulation. Serve immediately over cooked fruits.

sablé [sah-BLAY] (see shortbread)

Saint-Honoré [sant-ohn-oh-RAY]
French origin. A circle of baked puff pastry with attached cream puffs.

Saint-Tropez [san-troh-PAY]
French origin. Make a brioche dough. Roll into a 12-inch circle, ½ inch thick. Sprinkle with sugar. Bake at 350°F until golden. Cool on rack. Slice in two, horizontally. Spread thick crème pâtissière on bottom circle. Top with second circle. Sprinkle with powdered sugar.

savarin [sav-uh-RAHN]
French origin. Dissolve ¼ oz fresh yeast in ⅓ cup milk and heat. Mix 1¾ cup flour, 3 eggs, 1 teaspoon sugar, and the milk/yeast mix. Knead. Add 5 tablespoons fresh butter. Allow to rise. Place in savarin molds. Allow to rise again. Glaze with egg yolks. Bake at 350°F until golden. Unmold. Saturate with rum syrup. Serve at room temperature.

savoiardi [sav-oh-YAHR-dee] (see ladyfingers)

schwarzwälder kirschtorte [SHVARTZ-val-der KERSH-tor-tuh] (see black forest cake)

scone
Many variations. Whisk 2 cups flour, ¼ sugar, 2 teaspoons baking powder, salt, ⅓ cup butter, 1 egg, and vanilla. Knead dough. Roll out thick. Cut with cookie cutter. Bake on silicone mat at 375°F.

Desserts

shoofly pie

American origin (Pennsylvania). Line pie pan with flaky pastry. Mix 1 cup flour, ⅔ cup brown sugar, ¼ cup butter, 1 cup molasses, 1 egg, 1 teaspoon baking soda, and 1 cup boiling hot water. Pour mix into pie crust. Bake at 350°F until set.

shortbread

Mix 2 cups flour, salt, 1 cup butter, and ½ cup confectioners' sugar. Roll out dough. Cut with cookie cutter. Bake on silicone mat at 350°F.

shortbread pastry

Make a dough with 1¼ cups flour, ⅓ cup sugar, salt, 4 oz butter, and 1 egg.

shortcake

American origin. Roll out shortcake dough into 2-inch rounds. Bake at 450°F for 10 minutes. Marinate strawberries or other fruits with sugar. (If desired, add rum or Grand Marnier.) To assemble, halve the shortcake rounds, top with fruit mix, and then with whipped cream.

shortcake dough

American origin. Mix 2 cups flour, 2½ teaspoons baking powder, ½ teaspoon salt, 6 tablespoons butter, and ¾ cup milk. Knead.

slump

American origin. Mix fruits with sugar and water. Cook like a marmalade. Add spoonfuls of slump dough to the mix. Cover and steam for 30 minutes.

slump dough

American origin. Mix 1½ cups flour, 2 teaspoons baking powder, and ½ teaspoon salt. Add 1 cup milk and 4 tablespoons butter.

soufflé [soo-FLAY]

Start with thick Béchamel sauce or pastry cream. Season accordingly with savory or sweet garnish, salt, and pepper. Add 2 egg yolks per cup of sauce or cream. Fold in 1 whipped egg white for each egg yolk. Pour into butter, sugar- or breadcrumb-coated ramekins. Bake at 375°F until risen and golden brown on top.

souffléed omelet

Beat egg yolks and sugar. Whisk egg whites. Fold into the egg yolk and sugar mixture. Sauté until browned on the outside and soft and creamy on the inside. Fold or leave flat. (If desired, fill with fruit or preserves.)

Desserts

sponge cake
  Similar to genoise. Beat 6 egg yolks and 1 cup sugar into a thick
  ribbon. Flavor with liquor or extract. Fold in 1 cup sifted flour. Then
  fold in 6 whipped egg whites. Bake in cake pan at 350°F until golden
  and cooked through. Cool on rack. Serve warm, at room temperature,
  or freeze for later use.

spotted dick
  British origin. Make a pastry dough with suet by pulsing together 1½
  cups flour, ⅓ cup sugar, 1 tablespoon baking powder, salt,
  8 tablespoons milk, and 1 cup rendered suet. Knead dry currants
  and raisins into dough. Shape into a cylinder and steam or boil until
  cooked through. Slice and serve at room temperature with custard.

spotted dog (see spotted dick)

sticky pudding
  Simmer 1 cup dates. Beat 4 oz butter with ¼ cup brown sugar. Add
  1 egg, 1 cup self-rising flour, and salt. Add dates. Bake in individual
  ramekins or round cake pan at 350°F until cooked through and golden.

summer pudding
  British origin. Cook summer fruits such as raspberries or strawberries
  with sugar. Layer bread slices in an oven dish. Pour in stewed summer
  fruits. Chill overnight. Unmold and serve cold.

sweet flaky pastry
  Make a dough with 2½ cups flour, ¾ cup sugar, 4 oz butter, salt to
  taste, and enough cold water to bind.

sweet potato pie
  American origin (Southern). Line a pie pan with flaky pastry. Make
  custard with 3 eggs, 2 cups sweet potato purée, 1½ cups cream,
  ½ cup sugar, ⅓ cup brown sugar, cinnamon, nutmeg, allspice, and
  salt. Pour custard into pie crust. Bake at 325°F until custard is set.

tapioca pudding
  Soak tapioca in 3 cups of milk. Whisk in 2 egg yolks, salt, ⅓ cup
  sugar, and vanilla bean. Slowly cook until thick and creamy.

tart
  Line pie pan with flaky pastry or shortbread pastry. Poke holes in pastry
  with a fork. Bake at 350°F until dried and light golden. Cool. Fill with
  pastry cream. Top with uncooked fresh fruits such as berries or kiwis. Chill.

tarte Tatin [tahrt ta-TEHN]

French origin. Make a caramel with butter and sugar in skillet. Cook quartered apples in the caramel to soften. Arrange apples in a tight circle in the skillet. Cover with flaky pastry. Tuck at the sides. Bake at 350°F until crust is dark golden. Rest and cool. Flip skillet over a dish to remove.

tipsy cake

1. English version. (see trifle)
2. Scottish version. Spread sponge cake with jam. Soak in brandy. Top with meringue. Bake at 350°F.
3. American version. Many variations. Soak sponge cake with whiskey. Top with thick custard. Top with another layer of whiskey-soaked sponge cake. Serve at room temperature.

tiramisu [ti-ruh-MEE-soo]

Italian origin. Dip ladyfingers in espresso and arrange at bottom of cake dish. Top with mascarpone folded in with egg yolks, sugar, and vanilla. Chill. To serve, unmold and cut into square portions. Dust with cocoa powder and serve.

torrone [tor-ROHN-eh] (see turrón)

trifle [TRI-fuhl]

English origin. In a glass bowl, assemble sponge cake or soaked ladyfingers, fresh fruits, and thick custard. Top with whipped cream.

Tropezienne [troh-pay-ZYEN] (see Saint-Tropez)

truffles

Make a thick ganache. Shape into bite-sized balls. Roll in cocoa powder. Serve chilled or at room temperature.

tuiles [TWEEL]

French origin. Mix ⅓ cup orange juice, ¼ cup Grand Marnier, 1¼ cups sugar, 7 tablespoons butter, 2 cups chopped almonds, and 1 cup flour. Press round shapes on silicone mat. Bake at 350°F until golden brown. Cool cookies on rolling pin to achieve curved shape.

turnover

Roll out puff pastry into 11-inch square. Place on silicone mat. Fill with thick apple sauce and fold over to make triangle. Slit the top 3 times. Tighten the edges. Brush with egg wash. Bake at 400°F until golden brown.

Desserts

turrón [too-ROHN]
Heat 1⅓ cups honey. Stir in beaten egg whites and cook until toffee-like consistency. Add 3½ oz hazelnuts and 8 oz almonds. Reserve. Spread edible rice paper on sheet pan. Spread mixture on rice paper. Cool and cut to serve.

upside-down cake
American origin. Cook butter and brown sugar in a cast-iron skillet. Add fruits such as pineapple, plums, peaches, or apricots. Mix together 2 eggs, 8 tablespoons buttermilk, 1 cup flour, ¾ cup sugar, ¾ teaspoon baking powder, ¼ teaspoon of baking soda, 6 tablespoons butter, and salt to taste. (If desired, add vanilla and cinnamon.) Pour over fruits in the skillet. Bake 350°F for 45 minutes.

upside-down pie
American origin. Toss quartered apples or other fruits with brown sugar and spices such as cinnamon and nutmeg. (If desired, add nuts such as pecans.) Line pie pan with flaky pastry. Add apples. Cover with another flaky pastry crust. Tuck sides. Bake at 350°F until crust is dark golden. Rest and cool. Flip pie pan over a dish to remove.

Yorkshire pudding
Make a batter with 1 tablespoon butter, 4¾ oz flour, salt, 2 eggs and 1 cup milk. Bake in popover tins at 400°F until puffed up, dried, and golden brown. Serve immediately.

yule log
Prepare sponge cake in sheet pan. Remove and roll out when still warm. Spread on buttercream and roll up tight. Decorate with buttercream as if cake is a wooden log. Chill.

zabaglione [zah-bahl-YOH-neh] (see sabayon)

zuppa inglese [ZOO-pah een-GLAY-seh]
Italian origin. Many variations. Similar to triffle. In a cake pan, layer sponge cake or ladyfingers soaked in liquor and lemon-flavored pastry cream. (If desired, add chocolate pastry cream.) Chill. Unmold. (If desired, top with whipped cream and toasted almonds.)

Desserts